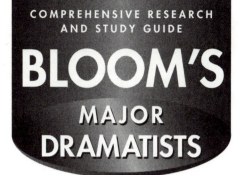

COMPREHENSIVE RESEARCH
AND STUDY GUIDE

BLOOM'S
MAJOR
DRAMATISTS

Shakespeare's Romances

EDITED AND WITH AN
INTRODUCTION BY HAROLD BLOOM

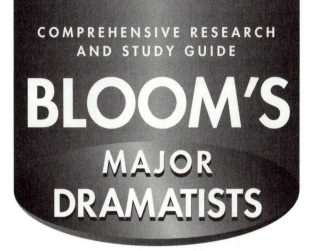

COMPREHENSIVE RESEARCH
AND STUDY GUIDE

BLOOM'S
MAJOR
DRAMATISTS

Shakespeare's Romances

EDITED AND WITH AN INTRODUCTION
BY HAROLD BLOOM

© 2000 by Chelsea House Publishers, a division of Main Line Book Co.

Introduction © 2000 by Harold Bloom

Printed and bound in the United States of America.

First Printing
1 3 5 7 9 8 6 4 2

Library of Congress Cataloging-in-Publication Data
Shakespeare's romances : comprehensive research and study guide /
    edited and with an introduction by Harold Bloom.
        p.   cm. — (Bloom's major dramatists)
    Includes biographical references (p.   ) and index.
    ISBN 0-7910-5244-3 (hc)
    1. Shakespeare, William, 1564–1616—Tragicomedies—Examinations
Study   guides.   I. Bloom, Harold.   II. Series
PR2981.S49   1999
822.3'3--dc21   99–29303
                                                              CIP

Chelsea House Publishers
1974 Sproul Road, Suite 400
Broomall, PA 19008-0914

The Chelsea House world wide web address is
www.chelseahouse.com

Contributing Editor: Janyce Marson

Contents

User's Guide

This volume is designed to present biographical, critical, and bibliographical information on the author's best-known or most important works. Following Harold Bloom's editor's note and introduction are a detailed biography of the playwright, discussing major life events and important literary accomplishments. A plot summary of each play follows, tracing significant themes, patterns, and motifs in the work.

A selection of critical extracts, derived from previously published material from leading critics, analyzes aspects of each work. The extracts consist of statements from the author, if available, early reviews of the work, and later evaluations up to the present. A bibliography of the author's writings (including a complete list of all works written, cowritten, edited, and translated), a list of additional books and articles on the author and his or her work, and an index of themes and ideas in the author's writings conclude the volume.

~

Harold Bloom is Sterling Professor of the Humanities at Yale University and Henry W. and Albert A. Berg Professor of English at the New York University Graduate School. He is the author of over 20 books and the editor of more than 30 anthologies of literary criticism.

Professor Bloom's works include *Shelley's Mythmaking* (1959), *The Visionary Company* (1961), *Blake's Apocalypse* (1963), *Yeats* (1970), *A Map of Misreading* (1975), *Kabbalah and Criticism* (1975), and *Agon: Toward a Theory of Revisionism* (1982). *The Anxiety of Influence* (1973) sets forth Professor Bloom's provocative theory of the literary relationships between the great writers and their predecessors. His most recent books include *The American Religion* (1992), *The Western Canon* (1994), *Omens of Millennium: The Gnosis of Angels, Dreams, and Resurrection* (1996), and *Shakespeare: The Invention of the Human* (1998), a finalist for the 1998 National Book Award.

Professor Bloom earned his Ph.D. from Yale University in 1955 and has served on the Yale faculty since then. He is a 1985 MacArthur Foundation Award recipient, served as the Charles Eliot Norton Professor of Poetry at Harvard University in 1987–88, and has received honorary degrees from the universities of Rome and Bologna. In 1999, Professor Bloom received the prestigious American Academy of Arts and Letters Gold Medal for Criticism.

Currently, Harold Bloom is the editor of numerous Chelsea House volumes of literary criticism, including the series BLOOM'S NOTES, BLOOM'S MAJOR SHORT STORY WRITERS, BLOOM'S MAJOR POETS, MAJOR LITERARY CHARACTERS, MODERN CRITICAL VIEWS, MODERN CRITICAL INTERPRETATIONS, AND WOMEN WRITERS OF ENGLISH AND THEIR WORKS.

Editor's Note

Each of the two dozen or so Critical Extracts has a unique value, and I have not space here to delineate this.

I particularly commend Howard Felperin on *Pericles,* and Peter Alexander and Arthur Kirsch on *Cymbeline,* while Stephen Orgel seems to me of great interest on *The Winter's Tale.*

With *The Tempest,* the reader is offered a choice between older, metaphysical concerns in Don Cameron Allen and Theodore Spencer, and the brave new world of politicized historicism in Jonathan Bate and S. J. Greenblatt.

Introduction

HAROLD BLOOM

An unfortunate critical tradition, now too prevalent to be overthrown, has named this fourfold of late Shakespearean dramas his "romances." Actually very different from one another, they are essentially comedies, perhaps tragicomedies. Though all of them have visionary elements, none is as extreme as *A Midsummer Night's Dream* or *Macbeth* in relying upon the supernatural. Because these "late romances" have the misleading reputation as being works of an ultimate reconciliation, they tend to be inadequately performed, with their comic ethos thrown away, that being the particular fate now of *The Tempest.*

Pericles, the earliest of these plays, essentially is a pageant or processional, while *Cymbeline* seems to me an extravagant self-parody, in which Shakespeare recalls earlier triumphs largely to mock them. *The Winter's Tale* is even more a knowing illusion, at once a passionate celebration of eros, and a paean to the horrible glories of sexual jealousy. Though *The Tempest* is now widely acted and written about as a postcolonial farce, it seems to me Shakespeare's comic version of the Faust story, with Prospero supplanting Marlowe's Dr. Faustus, and Ariel taking the place of the Marlovian Mephistopheles.

Once we regard these four plays as comedies or tragicomedies, their supposed common features and themes tend to vanish. Shakespeare, a naturally comic genius even in *Hamlet* and in *Antony and Cleopatra,* is furthest from comedy in *Othello* and *Macbeth. King Lear,* most tragic of tragedies, is also wildly grotesque, transcending the limits of laughter in the Fool's apocalyptic ironies. Shakespeare returns greatly to comedy in *The Winter's Tale* and *The Tempest,* as much triumphs of irony and wit as are *As You Like It* and *Twelfth Night,* or in a darker mode, *Measure for Measure.* Once you realize that Caliban, despite his cowardly poignance, is a comic villain and not a heroic West Indian Freedom Fighter, then the laughter of *The Tempest* returns, though this humor is now in political exile from our stages.

What matters most about these misnamed "romances" is their greatest strength, invention, which Dr. Johnson rightly considered the essence of poetry. The brothel scenes in *Pericles* juxtapose the impregnable Marina with the amiably bewildered bawds, who want only to get on with their business, mixing pleasure and profit with venereal illness and casual death. *Cymbeline,* which obsessively cannot cease from Shakespearean self-parody, nevertheless centers upon Imogen, who joins Rosalind, Portia, and Helena among the playwright's most delightful and humanly impressive women. *The Winter's Tale* is most memorable for its contraries, the murderous insanity of Leontes's sexual jealousy, and the loving splendor of his daughter, Perdita, a new Prosperina renewing the fertility of the earth. Add Autolycus, sublime singer of thievery, and you have a world of interest and value manifested in a new kind of comedy.

That comedy, which as yet we scarcely understand, triumphs in *The Tempest,* in the contrast between Prospero and his enemies, and in the more radical disjunction between Prospero's ally, Ariel, and his outcast adopted child, Caliban. Politicizing *The Tempest* has merely obscured its comic splendor, but Shakespeare, greatest of entertainers as of poets, never can be obscured for long.

Biography of
William Shakespeare

William Shakespeare was born in Stratford-on-Avon in April 1564 into a family of some prominence. His father, John Shakespeare, was a glover and merchant of leather goods, who earned enough to marry the daughter of his father's landlord, Mary Arden, in 1557. John Shakespeare was a prominent citizen in Stratford, and at one point, he served as an alderman and bailiff.

Shakespeare presumably attended the Stratford grammar school, where he would have received an education in Latin, but he did not go on to either Oxford or Cambridge universities. Little is recorded about Shakespeare's early life; indeed, the first record of his life after his christening is of his marriage to Anne Hathaway in 1582 in the church at Temple Grafton, near Stratford. He would have been required to obtain a special license from the bishop as security that there was no impediment to the marriage. Peter Alexander states in his book *Shakespeare's Life and Art* that marriage at this time in England required neither a church nor a priest or, for that matter, even a document—only a declaration of the contracting parties in the presence of witnesses. Thus, it was customary, though not mandatory, to follow the marriage with a church ceremony.

Little is known about William and Anne Shakespeare's marriage. Their first child, Susanna, was born in May 1583, and twins, Hamnet and Judith Shakespeare, in 1585. Later on, Susanna married Dr. John Hall, but the younger daughter, Judith, remained unmarried. When Hamnet died in Stratford in 1596, the boy was only eleven years old.

There is no record of Shakespeare's activities for the seven years after the birth of his twins, but by 1592 he was in London working as an actor. He was also apparently well-known as a playwright, for reference is made of him by his contemporary, Robert Greene, in *A Groatsworth of Wit*, as "an upstart crow."

Several companies of actors were in London at this time. Shakespeare may have had connection with one or more of them before 1592, but there is no record that tells us definitely. However, he had a long association with the most famous and successful troupe, the Lord Chamberlain's Men. (When James I came to the throne in 1603, after Elizabeth's death, the troupe's name changed to the King's Men.) In 1599 the Lord Chamberlain's Men provided the financial backing for the construction of their own theatre, the Globe.

The Globe was begun by a carpenter named James Burbage and finished by his two sons, Cuthbert and Robert. To escape the jurisdiction of the Corporation of London, which was composed of conservative Puritans who opposed the theatre's "licentiousness," James Burbage built the Globe just outside London, in the Liberty of Holywell, beside Finsbury Fields. This also meant that the Globe was safer from the threats that lurked in London's crowded streets, like plague and other diseases, as well as rioting mobs. When James Burbage died in 1598, his sons completed the Globe's construction. Shakespeare played a vital role, financially and otherwise, in the construction of the theater, which was finally occupied some time before May 16, 1599.

Shakespeare acted with the Globe's company of actors; he was also a shareholder and eventually became the troupe's most important playwright. The company included London's most famous actors, who inspired the creation of Shakespeare's well-known characters such as Hamlet and Lear, as well as his clowns and fools.

In his early years, however, Shakespeare did not confine himself to the theatre. He also composed some mythological-erotic poetry, such as *Venus and Adonis* and *The Rape of Lucrece*, both of which were dedicated to the earl of Southampton. Shakespeare was successful enough that in 1597 he was able to purchase his own home in Stratford, New Place. He could even call himself a gentleman, for his father had been granted a coat of arms.

By 1598 Shakespeare had written some of his most famous works, such as *Romeo and Juliet*, *The Comedy of Errors*, *A Midsummer Night's Dream*, *The Merchant of Venice*, *Two Gentleman of Verona*, and *Love's Labor Lost*, as well as his historical plays: *Richard II*, *Richard III*, *Henry IV*, and *King John*. Somewhere around the turn of the century, Shakespeare wrote his romantic comedies, *As You Like It*, *Twelfth Night*, and *Much Ado About Nothing*, as well as *Henry V*, the last of his history plays in the Prince Hal series. During the next ten years he wrote his great tragedies: *Hamlet*, *Macbeth*, *Othello*, *King Lear*, and *Antony and Cleopatra*.

At this time, the theatre was burgeoning in London; the public took an avid interest in drama, the audiences were large, the plays demonstrated an enormous range of variety, and playwrights competed for approval. By 1613, however, the rising tide of Puritanism had changed the theatre. With the desertion of the theatres by the middle classes, the acting companies were compelled to depend more on the aristocracy, which also meant that they now had to cater to a more sophisticated audience.

Perhaps this change in London's artistic atmosphere contributed to Shakespeare's reasons for leaving London after 1612. His retirement from the theatre is sometimes thought to be evidence that his artistic skills were waning. During this time, however, he wrote *The Tempest* and *Henry VIII.* He also wrote the tragicomedies, *Pericles, Cymbeline,* and *The Winter's Tale.* These were thought to be inspired by Shakespeare's personal problems, and have sometimes been considered proof of his greatly diminished abilities.

However, so far as biographical facts indicate, the circumstances of his life at this time do not imply any personal problems. He was in good health, financially secure, and enjoyed an excellent reputation. Indeed, although he was settled in Stratford at this time, he made frequent visits to London, enjoying and participating in events at the royal court, directing rehearsals, and attending to other business matters.

In addition to his brilliant and enormous contributions to the theatre, Shakespeare remained a poetic genius throughout the years, publishing a well-renowned and critically acclaimed sonnet cycle in 1609. Shakespeare's contribution to this popular poetic genre are all the more amazing in his break with contemporary notions of subject matter. Shakespeare idealized the beauty of man as an object of praise and devotion (rather than the Petrarchan tradition of the idealized, unattainable woman). In the same spirit of breaking with tradition, Shakespeare also treated themes which hitherto had been considered off limits—the dark, sexual side of a woman as opposed to the Petrarchan ideal of a chaste and remote love object. He also expanded the sonnet's emotional range, including such emotions as delight, pride, shame, disgust, sadness, and fear.

When Shakespeare died in 1616, no collected edition of his works had ever been published, although some of his plays had been printed in separate unauthorized editions. (Some of these were taken from his manuscripts, some from the actors' prompt books, and others were re-constructed from memory by actors or spectators.) In 1623, two members of the King's Men, John Hemings and Henry Condell, published a collection of all the plays they considered to be authentic, the First Folio.

Included in the First Folio is a poem by Shakespeare's contemporary Ben Jonson, an outstanding playwright and critic in his own right. Jonson paid tribute to Shakespeare's genius, proclaiming his superiority to what previously had been held as the models for literary excellence–the Greek and Latin writers. "Triumph, my Britain, thou hast one to show / To whom all scenes of Europe homage owe. / He was not of an age, but for all time!"

Jonson was the first to state what has been said so many times since. Having captured what is permanent and universal to all human beings at all times, Shakespeare's genius continues to inspire us—and the critical debate about his works never ceases. ❀

Plot Summary of
Pericles

The source for *Pericles* is a remote eastern Mediterranean folk-tale that eventually evolved into the story known as *Pericles, Prince of Tyre.* Although the time of its original composition is unknown, it was probably first written in Greece around the third century because it contains elements of Greek romances written by such ancient writers as Heliodorus, Longus, and Achilles Tatius. Some Latin manuscripts of similar stories date back to the eighth or ninth century. Prior to its written form, however, the story of *Pericles, Prince of Tyre* was probably part of an oral tradition, existing in the form of several stories and thus communal in authorship. The fable would have wandered from teller to listener around the marketplace of the Levant for a time span of more than one thousand years.

The shared elements of the early versions of the story all contain a hero named Apollonius who has a daughter named Tarsia (or a very similar name). Tarsia's wanderings are woven into various episodic tales, including many amusing riddles or seemingly puzzling situations that all end in the reunion of father and daughter. By all accounts, the story of Apollonius was enormously popular, a popularity that may be due to various elements that captivated its audiences, namely, a series of episodes or small stories within a larger structure, an exotic setting, dramatic reversals of fortune, and the pathos of the hero's undeserved suffering. The audience's sympathy and identification with the hero is heightened by the fact that though Apollonius is born a prince, he nevertheless must strive to overcome difficult obstacles and demonstrate strength and patience in order to recover his rightful inheritance and status in the world.

So popular was the story that it survived into the Middle Ages, appealing to a populace that was taught by the Church to understand the sufferings of this world in terms of a higher and more ennobling reward in heaven. The tale's popularity continued to grow throughout the Renaissance. Shakespeare would have read the two major written sources of this legend: Gower's *Confessio Amantis* (1390s) and Laurence Twine's *The Patterne of Painefull Adventures* (c. 1594).

The *Confessio Amantis* concerns the confession of a lover, named Amans, who seeks for help from Venus in examining his conscience.

To address Venus, Amans goes to one of her priests, Genius. The examination of Amans's conscience requires the lover to tell the story of his behavior and experiences in love. Within the *Confessio Amantis* is the story of "Apollonis, Prince of Tyre," which is used to instruct the reader against the dangers of incestuous love. Furthermore, the fact that Genius, the narrator of the *Confessio Amantis,* clearly enjoys the role of storyteller surely convinced Shakespeare to use Gower as the dramatic narrator and ancient storyteller of *Pericles.*

Twine's novel, *The Patterne of Painefull Adventures,* tells the "variable Historie of the strange accidents that befell unto Prince Apollonius. . . . Wherein the uncertaintie of this world, and the fickle state of mans life are lively described." Although Gower is the more influential of the two Renaissance sources, Twine's influence is especially strong in Act IV of Shakespeare's *Pericles,* where, for instance, Shakespeare confines the scene in Miteline to the brothel rather than Twine's street scenes where Tharsia (Marina in *Pericles*) is sold in the market and then paraded through the streets to attract the attention of the public.

The period from April to December 1607 were plague years in London (as were the summer and autumn of 1608), and consequently, the theatres were closed. Shakespeare's *Pericles* was performed no later than 1608, probably sometime during the first six months of that year, as recorded by the visiting Venetian ambassador, Zorzi Giustinian.

In **Act I,** Gower, like the chorus in ancient tragedy, sets forth what the audience is about to see, namely how the young Pericles will be tested for his suitability to win the hand of the daughter of King Antiochus. "To seek her as a bedfellow . . . Which to prevent he made a law . . . That whoso asked her for his wife, / His riddle told not, lost his life." That test is a fearful one, requiring an extraordinary human demonstration of courage as the hero must either successfully answer the riddle or else forfeit his own life. Furthermore, the most frightening aspect of that riddle is its strong suggestion that Antiochus has an incestuous love for his daughter. Pericles correctly reads and understands the dire implication of the riddle and flees from this unspeakable crime. Antiochus's response is to send one of his courtiers, Thaliard, to find Pericles and kill him. At the same time, Pericles consults with Helicanus, a trusted lord of Tyre, and they decide to flee their own country and travel the world. Upon arriving at Tyre and learning of this plan, Thaliard tells his own version of the story to Antiochus—that Pericles has escaped by boat and will die at sea.

When Pericles arrives by sea at Tharsus, he finds the city stricken by a famine. Cleon, the governor of Tharsus, and his wife, Dionyza, are bemoaning the tragic state of their town. When they hear of Pericles' arrival, Cleon and Dionyza initially expect that this stranger will take advantage of their town's beleaguered status and appropriate Tharsus for his own personal gain. Instead, true to his heroic nature, Pericles demonstrates sympathy for their plight, and he gives them corn to feed their people.

In **Act II**, a "dumb show" (a pantomime or dramatic performance that conveys meaning by gesture only) is hidden in Gower's introduction, which shows Pericles, when learning by letter that Thaliard has ordered him killed, setting sail in great haste on the stormy seas. Three fishermen advise Pericles that a tournament has been arranged so that he may compete with the other suitors to win the hand of the benign King Simonides' daughter. Further, by a strange coincidence of fortune, the fishermen have captured a rusty suit of armor that Pericles recognizes as having belonged to his father. With this lucky find, Pericles is encouraged to attempt the tournament.

Ironically, when he does, he appears the least worthy of all the suitors. Simonides remarks, "He's but a country gentleman: / H'as done no more than other knights have done / H'as broken a staff or so, so let it pass." Nevertheless, the hero wins the day and the hand of Thaisa, Simonides' daughter.

In the beginning of **Act III,** Gower again summarizes the events, now telling of the marriage and the conception of a child: "Brief, he must hence depart to Tyre; / His queen, with child makes her desire - / . . . Lychorida her nurse she takes." Pericles now learns that Antiochus and his daughter are dead and that the men of Tyre will give the crown to Pericles' trusted advisor, Helicanus, if the hero does not return. Thus, Pericles leaves for Tyre with his wife Thaisa, who is about to give birth. Along the way, they are caught in a turbulent storm that unmercifully rocks their ship and causes Pericles to rail against fate when he learns that Thaisa has died giving birth to a daughter. Thaisa's terrible fate arouses tremendous suspicion from the crew, who demand that her body be cast in the ocean.

In another turn of fortune, Thaisa's body, which has been sealed in a chest, washes ashore at Ephesus and is brought to a healer named Cerimon. Cerimon uses special potions, "the blest infusions that dwells

/ In vegetives, in metals, stones; and can speak of the / Disturbances that nature works and of her cures," and is able to revive the "deceased" Thaisa: "I pray you give her air: / Gentlemen, this queen will live: / Nature awakes, a warmth breathes out of her." Pericles, however, is unaware of this strange reversal of fortune and thus stops at Tharsus to leave his new daughter, Marina, and her nurse, Lychorida, to the care of Cleon and Dionyza.

As Gower tells us in the beginning of **Act IV,** many years have gone by, during which time Pericles has become the ruler of Tyre, and Marina in Tharsus has grown into a beautiful, virtuous, and talented young woman. Indeed, her beauty and intelligence far outshine Dionyza's daughter, a fact which provokes the jealous Queen Dionyza to plot Marina's murder. Thus, while the unsuspecting Marina is gathering flowers for her nurse's grave, Leonine, the man who is to murder her, tells her of her danger, though he remains determined to carry out the deed.

Once again, fate intervenes and Marina is rescued by pirates, who bring her to Mytilene and sell her to a bawd who in turn tries to sell Marina's chastity to the highest bidder. But Marina, very much like a saint (another fact that demonstrates why the legend of Pericles was popular in the Middle Ages) remains steadfast while in the brothel, preaching virtue to her would-be clients, In the end, she triumphs over the Bawd and the evil Boult (servant to Bawd's husband Pander), whose money-making attempts have been completely thwarted.

While all this is going on, Pericles is once again provided with a dumb show in which he is advised of his daughter's death. He reacts with a vow to cut his hair and live in perpetual sorrow.

In **Act V,** Lysimachus, the Governor of Mytilene greets Pericles's newly-arrived ship. Pericles has now been suffering from a deep depression for three months. "I am great with woe, and shall deliver weeping" he tells Lysimachus, who then summons Marina to minister to him with her healing abilities (in the Middle Ages, this was considered another important saintly power). When Pericles asks her to tell her story, he discovers the daughter he has long been separated from, and overwhelmed with joy, he falls asleep and dreams of the mythological goddess Diana who, in the dream, directs him to attend her temple at Ephesus and give thanks for his good fortune. In mythology Diana is the goddess of chastity, the hunt, and the moon, a mythological reference that runs parallel with his chaste daughter Marina.

When he does arrive at the temple, the final joyful reversal of fortune occurs and he is reunited with his beloved Thaisa who is now serving as Diana's high priestess. Thus, the play ends much like a medieval morality play. Faith, courage, and virtuous living are rewarded, and evil punished through the intervention of avenging gods who bring about the death of Cleon and Dionyza. Their demise is announced by Gower who ends the play with the final epilogue. ❀

List of Characters in
Pericles

Antiochus, King of Antioch presents Pericles with a riddle, the solution of which reveals the King to be guilty of an incestuous love for his daughter. Interestingly, his daughter's name is never mentioned in the play. When Pericles correctly solves the riddle of how a man could simultaneously be father, son, and husband, he flees in abject horror. Upon learning that Pericles has fled, Antiochus demonstrates his vindictive nature by sending a courtier to find Pericles and kill him.

The adventures of **Pericles, Prince of Tyre** form the focal point and unity of the play bearing his name, with all subsequent characters being subordinate to him. The basic narrative pattern in his romantic adventures involves the love for and loss of an idealized young woman and his eventual compensation for that loss. In Act I, Gower, like the chorus in ancient tragedy, sets forth what the audience is about to see, namely how the young Pericles will be tested, as are all other amorous contenders, for his suitability to win the hand of the daughter of King Antiochus. That test consists in answering a riddle and, when Pericles correctly understands the dire implication of Antiochus's incestuous relationship with his daughter, the young hero flees from this unspeakable crime. Antiochus responds by sending one of his courtiers to kill Pericles. Pericles embarks on a journey in which his true mettle is tested. Those trials include a tempestuous sea voyage and his arrival at Tharsus, the famine-stricken city of Cleon, the governor, and his wife, Dionyza. Later on, in one of several reversals of fortune, Pericles wins a tournament and the hand of Thaisa whom he is to marry. Though she appears to have died after giving birth to their daughter Marina, their family is reunited at the end of the play.

Marina, daughter to Pericles and Thaisa, is more of a beautiful, intelligent, and virtuous "type" of woman rather than a distinct personality. Aided by Diana, goddess of chastity, Marina is made to endure several severe tests of her courage and commitment and in so doing demonstrates a graceful acceptance of her trials and offers the hope of transcendence beyond the evil of this world. When Marina is sold to a brothel, she behaves very much like a saint (which again demonstrates why the legend of Pericles was popular in the Middle Ages) and instead preaches virtue to her would-be clients. Marina is also the symbol for hope in this world as she is the offspring of the fruitful marriage between Pericles and Thaisa and, thus, she signals the possibility of renewal.

Gower functions as the chorus of ancient drama in *Pericles,* commenting and moralizing on the events as they unfold. It has been suggested that the visual aspect of his character on stage was captivating to an audience who would recognize his striking costume as resembling an Elizabethan woodcut depicting a grim-faced character in a blue bonnet.

Cleon is governor of Tharsus. He is married to **Dionyza.** When Pericles arrives, Tharsus is being ravaged by famine. Shakespeare's characterization of Cleon and Dionyza is more pictorial than dramatic as it is through their dialogue that we get a vivid description of the famine. "Our cheeks and hollow eyes do witness it."

Lysimachus, governor of Mytilene, encounters the virtuous Marina in a brothel and attempts to undermine her resolve to remain chaste by impressing her with his power and political status.

Simonides is father of Thaisa. While Pericles does not at first meet Simonides' idealized concept of royalty, in time, he becomes very much in favor of his daughter's marriage to Pericles. Pericles wins his admiration through his gift of song, which Simonides acknowledges, "Sir, you are music's master."

Thaisa is daughter of Simonides and wife of Pericles. When she dies at sea while giving birth to their daughter Marina, her terrible fate arouses suspicion from the crew who demand that her body be cast in the ocean. However, in another turn of fortune, Thaisa's body, which has been sealed in a chest, washes ashore at Ephesus and brought to a healer named Cerimon. Cerimon using special potions found in vegetables, metals, and stones is able to revive Thaisa. When Pericles finally discovers that Thaisa is indeed alive, she is serving as Diana's high priestess. ✹

Critical Views on
Pericles

JOHN P. CUTTS ON PERICLES' VIOLENT NATURE

[John P. Cutts is the author of *Rich and Strange: A Study of Shakespeare's Last Plays* (1968) and *The Shattered Glass: A Dramatic Pattern in Shakespeare's Early Plays* (1968). In the excerpt below, Cutts argues that the hero's character is hardly a medieval exemplum of virtue but, rather, actually violent in nature.]

The play's opening, couched in medieval terminology, would surely have us consider "man's infirmities" (I.ch.3) to teach "frail mortality to know itself" (I.i.43) as a restorative. Any estimate of the play's total impact will certainly have to allow for the striking effect of the reincarnation of the medieval poet, but he is surely there not simply as a makeshift device for holding the play's sprawling action together, nor is he explainable by the colorful garb he wears suggestive of the quaintness of an archaic world. Gower's presence makes certain that the audience be made aware of mortality and man's infirmities. One would be hard pressed to find an exemplum in medieval drama that treated of its main figure as an "impeccably good man, a man without defect."

It is too easy to suggest that Pericles *accidentally* finds himself imbroiled in the discovery of Antiochus' incest, that he was innocent of any thought of wrongdoing when he approached Antiochus' court in the first place. It was hardly naïveté which led him to believe that he would be successful where many had failed before, that he would solve the riddle, Oedipus-like, win the daughter and become "son to great Antiochus" (I.i.27). He is in such a hurry to interrupt Antiochus, who is about to unfold all the dangers and difficulties, that when Antiochus merely addresses him as "Prince Pericles" Pericles rushes in with "That would be son to great Antiochus." But even if we were to allow him genuine innocence *before* he reaches Antiochus' court there can surely be no doubt of his impetuousness, his rashness, and his infatuation with moral danger once he is there. All the visible signs around him cannot be mistaken for anything but what they are, powerful indications of death on an insidious scale. Thinking "death no hazard in this enterprise" (I.i.5) he is little removed from Hamlet's "I'll speak to it, though hell itself should gape / And bid me hold my peace" because his "fate cries out," or from Faustus' "Ile conjure though I die therefore" or from Hotspur's "Albeit I make a hazard of my head" in his drunk-with-choler mood. "Thus ready for the way of life or death" (I.i.55) Pericles awaits the "sharpest blow" (I.i.56). Antiochus, like Mephistopheles with Faustus, does not equivocate on the mortal dangers inherent in Pericles' presumption. He points out the skulls of "sometimes famous princes" (I.i.35) which advise Pericles to desist "for going on death's net, whom none resist" (I.i.41). Pericles is in a House of Death and cannot but be sensitive of this fact. It is instructive, I think, to see how at the end of the play, where there are so many cross-references to Antiochus' court, Lysmachus will try to excuse his presence in a brothel house by claiming that he had not brought "[t]hither a corrupted mind" (IV.vi.103), but he protests too much his innocence for us to be convinced: "For me, be you thoughten / That I came with no ill intent: for to me / The very doors and windows savour vilely" (IV.vi.108–110). The same criterion he used in judging Marina— "Why, the house you dwell in proclaims you to be a creature of sale" (IV.vi.76–77)—must surely be exercised against himself. The house he has stepped into proclaims him to be a creature *buying*, and the Bawd, Pander and Boult evince no surprise at his seeking such a commodity.

Pericles' own terminology in the House of Death gives him away. To greet Antiochus' daughter, presented by the father as fit for "the embracements even of Jove himself" (I.i.8), as

> See, where she comes apparell'd like the spring
> Graces her subjects, and her thoughts the king
> Of every virtue gives renown to men!
> (I.i.13–15)

is to mistake the House of Death for the House of Life, and to invite consideration of Jove's immoral ventures rather than chaste behavior. Strangely enough Pericles himself sums up this confrontation with Antiochus' daughter by presuming "To taste the fruit of yon celestial tree" (I.i.22), thereby putting the whole situation in the context of Eden's tree of life or tree of death. Nor is this merely random rhetoric, for Antiochus' very next words place Pericles' quest in the context of Hercules' twelfth labor:

Before thee stands this fair Hesperides,
With golden fruit, but dangerous to be touch'd:
For death-like dragons here affright thee hard.
Her face, like heaven, enticeth thee to view.
                                      (I.i.28–31) ⟨ . . . ⟩

Like Guyon in Mammon's cave confronted with "a woman gorgeous gay, / And richly clad in robes of royaltye, / That neuer earthly Prince in such aray / His glory did enhaunce, and pompous pride display," and tempted to taste of the golden apples of this Proserpina's garden and to sit in her silver stool, Pericles is tempted by the magnificence, the wealth, and the power of Antiochus' daughter, but, unlike Guyon, he commits himself and asks for the passport, staking his whole "riches" (I.i.53) on the issue of the die. His easy couplet

For death remember'd should be like a mirror
Who tells us life's but breath, to trust it error
                                      (I.i.46–47)

could well be interpreted as a good man's recognition that he is dust and to dust shall return. But the mirror rhetoric is picked up again only a few lines later, after the anticlimax of the riddle, and heaven's countless eyes viewing man's acts are bidden not to peep through the blanket of the dark, but to hide their fires, to cloud their sights perpetually, not just because the revelation of the riddle causes Pericles to consider "There's nothing serious in mortality" as a consequence of Antiochus' action, but much more significantly if ironically because the "Fair glass of light" (I.i.77), Antiochus' daughter, in which he saw mirrored forth his conquest of magnificence, wealth, and power, has now been shattered. Instead of that glorious image of himself he is now freed to acknowledge that the Pandora he has opened "this glorious casket stor'd with ill" (I.i.78), the gift of all the gods to his way of thinking, and let loose in the world that which will work no peace, no rest, no comfort, until his sea voyage of life returns him a belief again in that innocence which his action in the court of Antiochus lost—his Marina, a symbol of his own personality (not just a symbol of the fruition of his marriage with Thaisa), and returns him a link again with human affairs, his purpose in life, his Thaisa—a symbol of his own personality, his link not just with his marriage partner but with his hold on life.

—John P. Cutts, "Pericles' 'Downright Violence.'" *Shakespeare Studies* 4 (1969): pp. 275–277.

[In the excerpt below, William O. Scott, a professor at the University of Kansas, discusses the importance of Marina's singing, most importantly that Pericles hears "heavenly music," within the context of Shakespeare's reworking of his two major sources for the play, Gower and Laurence Twine.]

The reunion of Pericles and Marina (V.i.42–220) is one of those almost miraculous scenes that we like to think of as the best of late Shakespeare. In his grief Pericles had renounced the world around him and refused to speak for three months, and he does not respond when Lysimachus greets and blesses him; only Marina can restore his interest in life. She is called because of her musical skill:

> She questionlesse with her sweet harmonie,
> And other chosen attractions, would allure
> And make a battrie through his defend [deafened] parts,
> Which now are midway stopt. . . .

Her singing does not seem to have an overt effect (line 81), but when she speaks to him just afterwards he responds enough to push her away and say "Hum, ha." Later he tells that this moment was "when I perceiu'd thee" (line 128). He listens as she says her griefs might equal his and tells of her "deriuation . . . from ancestors, / Who stood equiuolent with mightie Kings" (lines 91–92). He struggles to understand her words: "My fortunes, parentage, good parentage, / To equall mine, was it not thus, what say you?" His curiosity is aroused, and seeing her he is reminded of his wife and daughter; so he asks more questions and eventually, amid great feelings of wonder, the two recognize each other. It is Marina's powers and skills that accomplish this reunion, for if her music does not revive Pericles it at least prepares for his awakening, and she alone can compel him to listen to her. He listens, too, before he has much reason to wonder if she is his daughter.

Events run otherwise in the narrative sources of the play. In Laurence Twine's *Patterne of Painefull Adventures,* which gives the *Gesta Romanorum* version of the story, there is no silence but only an order by Apollonius (Pericles) that he not be disturbed; and Athanagoras (the counterpart of Lysimachus) is able to talk with Apollonius, who treats him courteously but expresses a wish to die. Apollonius' daughter Tharsia is called in because "she hath wisdom, & can move pleasant talke" and because Athanagoras recognizes the name of Tharsia's father. ⟨ . . . ⟩

The narrative in Grower's *Confessio Amantis* (VIII. 1629–1746) is at first closer to the play in this episode, but there are important divergences. Appolonius does keep silence when Atenagoras visits him on the ship, and he still shows no response when his daughter "harpeth many a laie" (line 1678). She changes her tactics, with only partial success:

> She falleth with hym unto wordes,
> And telleth him of sondrie bordes,
> And asketh of him demandes strange,
> Whereof she made his herte change,
> And to hir speche his eare he leyde
> And hath mervaile, of that she sayde. . . .
> But he for no suggestion,
> Whiche toward hym she couthe stere,
> He wolde not one worde answere.
> (lines 1683–1694)

He half-angrily bids her to go, she touches him, and he slaps her; but after a time he feels a heaven-sent natural kindness toward her ("he hir loveth kyndely / And yet he wist never why", lines 1715–1716) and asks her name and history, and her answers bring recognition. There is no suggestion that Atenagoras thinks he is bringing father and daughter together, and her musical ability is not singled out as a reason for her summoning. Gower's story, like the play, does make a point of the hero's silence. Music does not seem to reach him, again as in the play, but neither does he speak immediately after the singing as Pericles does. Though he is interested in his daughter's comic patter of jests, riddles, and proverbs, nothing that she does really brings him out of himself. Only by an inward prompting does he become curious about her, and they do not really converse freely, it seems, before he knows who she is. ⟨ . . . ⟩

Though Pericles' awakening is not that absurdly sudden or extreme and though we are told that he does not mark his daughter's music, singing is more important in the play and the emblem than in either narrative source. In Twine the man is not silent as he is in the play and the emblem, and the song really begins a series of riddles; in Gower the man's response does not immediately follow the song as in the play and the emblem but depends instead on riddles and divine urging.

The dramatist in looking at the emblem would have found several details that would suggest its relevance to Pericles' story: the man's melancholy and sleep, his refusal to speak (as in Gower), the playing of a harp (as in Gower—an unnamed instrument in Twine), and his awakening. In general the scene follows Gower more than Twine, but the playwright seems to have adapted Gower's narrative to give music some of the importance it has in the emblem. Yet the man's reaction in the emblem is made more plausible on stage by one softened detail from the two Apollonius stories: he gives a gentle push of rejection (less than a slap or a kick) before he listens and begins to speak.

The "diuine grace" of music and the power by which it "stirreth vp the soule to contemplation, comforteth the same, and maketh it heauenly as it were" is shown for us and made almost literal by an event that is not in any source: Pericles hears the "Most heauenly Musicke" of the spheres. This divine exaltation of music is the culmination of a pattern throughout the play. Antiochus' daughter, though a "faire Violl" that should have played "lawfule musicke", had been so debauched by evil that "Hell onely daunceth at so harsh a chime" (I.i.81–85). In the play as in the sources, Pericles wooes Thaisa with sweet music (II.v.25–28). The healing power of music, not named in the sources, helps Cerimon in his miraculous cure of Thaisa (III.ii.88–89). Marina escapes the brothel because she can "sing, weaue, sow, & dance" (IV.vi.194), and she is brought before Pericles to sing and revive him. Harmonious music accords with the love of man and woman or parent and child, and it betokens the power of good that revives the will to live.

—William O. Scott, "Another 'Herocial Devise' in *Pericles*." *Shakespeare Quarterly* 20 (1969): pp. 91–93.

Thelma N. Greenfield on Pericles' Resourcefulness

[Thelma N. Greenfield is the author of *The Induction in Elizabethan Drama* (1968) and *The Eye of Judgment: Reading the New Arcadia* (1968). In this excerpt, Greenfield goes against current criticism that sees Pericles as patient, and instead argues for a Pericles who is a wise and learned man, the Renaissance adaptation of the resourceful Greek traveler.]

Recent interpretations of *Pericles* present fairly consistently the view that the hero is a type of the patient man. We find, for example, this of J. F. Danby's: "In *Pericles* it is patience in adversity which is the dominating motif." D. A. Stauffer writes of the moral significance of the play, "Not only integrity, then, but patience, may make a man ruler over himself, and worthy of salvation." Kenneth Muir finds in *Pericles* "the triumph of patience." In his introduction to the New Arden edition, F. D. Hoeniger extensively develops the concept of patience as central both to the play's characterization of the hero and to its theme. Closely related to this patient hero is the "passive" and "resigned" Pericles of John Arthos and D. A. Traversi. Most influential among presentations of this view is J. M. S. Tompkins' "Why *Pericles?*" Tompkins finds Pericles more an example of patience than any other of Shakespeare's heroes and sees the conclusion of his story in terms of payment for this virtue: "As a character [Pericles] is almost static; he is the sport of fortune; the years and the great seas break over him; at last he turns his face to the wall, but in a despair that is silent and unrebellious; and then the gods restore to him the treasures they have reserved, and reward his patience."

The prospect of taking exception to such an array of opinion must give one pause, yet my own explanation of the evidence leads me to suggest that the patient Pericles be supplanted by the wise and learned one, the Renaissance descendent of the wily Greek traveler, a solver of riddles, a master of escape and incognito, skilled in the arts, and in his accomplishments and understanding a born ruler of men. This Pericles has a genius for coming out alive and, ultimately, on top, from the threats and disasters of a long, adventuresome life however much, like the storied philosopher, he can be bowed by inner griefs which his shrewdness and learning find no defence against. In all his wisdom, this Pericles willingly admits the power of the gods ("I am son and servant to your will") but he is a little short on faith in their benignity.

To proceed further with the wise and adroit but sometimes desolated Pericles, we must assess the evidence critics have set forth for the patient one. Although his patience is more often remarked upon than demonstrated, the evidence offered for the case is of two kinds, those instances where the word *patience* is spoken, implied, or enacted in the play—as when Helicanus or Lychorida or Marina adjures Pericles to be patient—and those instances where the play's relation to its sources shows by similarity or difference that Shakespeare's (or some other's) hand shaped the play toward the theme—as the impatience exhibited by Twine's Apollonius or the patience demonstrated by Plutarch's Pericles.

Hoeniger's arguments on the use or implications of the word, appearing importantly in the New Arden edition of the play, may be considered first. He begins with a comparison to *King Lear*, a play which surely comes to mind when we read *Pericles*. Hoeniger observes that Pericles (II.i and III.i) and King Lear (III.ii) react differently to the storms to which they are exposed—Lear encourages the storm, admits that he is its slave, and rebukes it, while Pericles patiently submits to it. This contrast bears a second look and doubtless goes deeper than Hoeniger indicates. Lear's immensely complicated responses to his storm are individual and varied, but clearly that storm becomes to the audience and to the hero an imaginative extension of Lear's own emotional state and simultaneously symbolic of his daughters' savagery. Pericles' storms, additional episodes in a series of adventures, have no such connections with pre-existent conflicts and inner tensions, and although the diction of Pericles' description of the turbulent elements may call Lear's speeches to mind, we cannot safely say that here are two characters reacting differently to the same thing. The storms in *Pericles,* completely external, lead the hero to new conditions and contemplations, unrelated, except as reversals, to his previous state. Pericles' reactions to the storm in Act II are those of a virtuous but thinking man: first, he says that man is helpless in the face of the angry heavens, and second, he designates himself as obedient, as man must be, to the powers above, and desires only a chance to be undisturbed. Interesting here is the use of logical patterns.

The passage, in full, reads as follows:

> Yet cease your ire, you angry stars of heaven!
> Wind, rain, and thunder, remember, earthly man
> Is but a substance that must yield to you:
> And I, as fits my nature, do obey you.
> Alas, the seas hath cast me on the rocks,
> Wash'd me from shore to shore, and left me breath
> Nothing to think on but ensuing death.
> Let it suffice the greatness of your powers
> To have bereft a prince of all his fortunes;
> And having thrown him from your wat'ry grave,
> Here to have death in peace is all he'll crave.
>
> (II.i.1–11)

Pericles, even in his extremity, thinks like a scholar: man must yield to you powers of nature; I am a man; therefore I obey you. You have left me breath only to think of death; therefore, I (who must obey you) think of death and having been deprived of a grave at sea desire only to die on land in peace. Lear, by contrast, speaks in imperatives, moral assessments, and the dawning of new perspectives. Pericles, distressed as he is, plays the learned disputant. He argues with the heavens even in praying: "Yet cease your ire . . . remember . . . let it suffice." The point of his argument is that since he has suitably cooperated in this demonstration of heavenly strength, he should now be tormented no further.

One sees here something other than patience: Pericles' tendency to rely on wit and to retreat in the face of odds greater than himself. Such was his method in the adventure with Antiochus and such will be his way of winning (almost accidentally) Thaisa at her father's court.

—Thelma N. Greenfield, "A Re-Examination of the 'Patient' *Pericles.*" *Shakespeare Survey* 3 (1967): pp. 51–53.

HOWARD FELPERIN ON SHAKESPEARE'S ARTISTIC POWER IN *PERICLES*

[Howard Felperin has written extensively on Shakespeare. His books include *Shakespearean Representation: Mimesis and Modernity in Elizabethan Tragedy* (1977) and *The Uses of the Canon: Elizabethan Literature and Contemporary Theory* (1990). In this excerpt, Felperin discusses the dramatic, visionary, and thematic integrity of *Pericles* and thereby argues against one of the critical theories that holds that Shakespeare evidenced a diminution of artistic power toward the end of his writing career.]

That the play is poetically coherent in detail and as serious as anything Shakespeare ever wrote has been eloquently demonstrated by Wilson Knight, and if certain potentialities were later developed at the expense of others (the same could be said in turn of each of the last plays, in fact, of every play in the canon), this is merely what we must expect from a dramatist who never simply repeated himself. The play's popularity with Shakespeare's audience should itself alert us to the existence of an internal coherence, then immediately intelligible and still accessible through the historical imagination.

The efficient causes of Shakespeare's final intuition of life as it suddenly emerges nearly full-blown in *Pericles* can never be known—was it the blooming of his daughter, the birth of his grandchild, a sense of impending old age, or a new calm of mind after the stormy affair with the Dark Lady? E. K. Chambers hazards this extreme theory:

> This profound cleavage in Shakespeare's mental history about 1607–1608 must have been due to some spiritual crisis the nature of which it is only possible dimly to conjecture; some such process as that which in the psychology of religion bears the name of conversion; or perhaps some sickness of the brain which left him an old man, freed at last from the fever of speculation and well disposed to spend the afternoon of life in unexacting and agreeable dreams. This latter hypothesis would help also to explain the marked change of style which accompanies the change of dramatic purpose in the romances.

It is indeed hard to imagine a virtually lobotomized Shakespeare writing the intricately constructed and harshly actualized plays of *Cymbeline* and *The Winter's Tale,* but the alternative theory of "religious conversion" commands more respect, and is, in fact, the avenue of approach taken by the most sympathetic modern interpreters. ⟨ . . . ⟩

The hypothesis that Shakespeare experienced some sort of religious conversion, intuition, vision, or inspiration about 1607–1608, which remained with him until the close of his career, is, of course, merely a critical convenience. It is useful only in so far as it illuminates the marked change of style and change of dramatic purpose in the last plays, to which Chambers alludes, and it is valid only in so far as it derives from the plays themselves. The change of style which *Pericles* announces seems all the more radical if we remember that it almost certainly follows *Coriolanus.* From the most naturalistically earthbound of the Tragedies, we move to the stagy fairy-tale of the first of the last plays. A lucid, chaste, Virgilian rhetoric gives place first to a gnomic, archaic, brittle verse and then, but the end of *Pericles,* to Shakespeare's final, magical speech-music; tight dramatic structure to slack, episodic, narrative structure; psychologically complex personalities to simple character-types; and so on. Rather than be baffled or exasperated we must assume that Shakespeare, at this point in his career, knew what he was doing: that the marked change in style is accounted for by a change in dramatic purpose, and the change in purpose, by a change in his poetic vision of life.

When Ancient Gower walked onto the stage as Chorus, a Jacobean audience would have been immediately aware of the archaism of the device. The convention of the poet as Chorus had been all but brushed aside by the momentum of increasing naturalism, and plays at this point in the development of the drama often began in mid-dialogue ("Tush, never tell me!", "Nay, but this dotage . . . "). The technique of poet as Chorus originates in the medieval religious drama, specifically in the saint's play, of which lamentably few in English have survived. The late-fifteenth-century *The Conversion of St. Paul* illustrates the technique; there, the *Poeta* introduces and recapitulates each scene, apologizes for breaks and leaps in the action, but, most importantly, acts as moral interpreter to the audience. Even if Shakespeare was unacquainted with this play, similar miracle or saint's plays were performed well into the late sixteenth century on their appropriate festival days. 〈 . . . 〉

Obviously Shakespeare would not deliberately cultivate an archaic medievalism at this stage in his work without very sophisticated ulterior motives. Gower's first speech is shot through with clues to Shakespeare's intentions:

> To sing a song that old was sung,
> From ashes ancient Gower is come
> Assuming man's infirmities,
> To glad your ear, and please your eyes.
> It hath been sung at festivals,
> On ember-eves and holy ales;
> And lords and ladies in their lives
> Have read it for restoratives:
> The purchase is to make men glorious,
> *Et bonum quo antiquius eo melius.*
> If you born in these latter times
> When wit's more ripe, accept my rimes . . .

The imitation of Gower's jingly rhymes, archaic diction, and simple-minded didacticism is itself skilful, and who but Shakespeare could have introduced so unobtrusively, yet purposefully, the main themes of the play, "man's infirmities", resurrection, and restoration, within the first eight lines? The humorous Latin tag, the contrast between "these latter times" and a "song that old was sung", a contrast embodied in the resurrected Gower himself, serve to surround the tale with an air of vague antiquity. "It hath been sung at festivals, / On ember-eves and holy ales"—all occasions in the Church calendar. In short, Shakespeare is telling us that the story we are about to witness will be a timeless parable for our spiritual enlightenment—like the miracle play—and that to learn from it we must unlearn our sophisticated notions of dramatic storytelling.

—Howard Felperin, "Shakespeare's Miracle Play." *Shakespeare Quarterly* 18 (1967): pp. 363–366.

John Arthos on *Pericles'* Romantic Narrative

[John Arthos has written extensively on Shakespeare and other Renaissance writers. His books include *Shakespeare: The Early Writings* (1972) and *Shakespeare's Use of Dream and Vision* (1977). In the excerpt below, Arthos discusses the way in which Shakespeare weaves a coherent, dramatic narrative from a play made up of "romantic" elements, such as the marvelous, brief episodes and the very sparse character development.]

One would begin with this, that the form of *Pericles*, deriving from extremely romantic material, must turn to dramatic use subjects and devices until now most effectively used in narrative. Romantic stories of a certain kind, crowded, fantastic, fabulous, would present the Elizabethan dramatist with a problem of particular interest and difficulty, for he would need to maintain the coherence and the culmination of power his audience had come to expect of comedies and tragedies alike, while developing another way of presenting a quite different kind of material. From a narrative parading marvels, where episodes are presented briefly and ended sharply, and in which characters are described simply and barely developed, he must make a play that will preserve the narrative's sense of wonder, develop the interest necessary for drama, and add the splendor of the stage. ⟨ . . . ⟩

The scene of *Pericles* moves from one strange sea-coast to another, from one city to another, one with barbaric customs, one wasted with starvation. Strangers cast up by the sea find armor to fit them and tournaments to win; pirates kidnap a princess. There is one adventure after another, most of them involving terrible misfortunes in outlandish places, guided in their sequence in the play, it would appear, by someone's belief in our insatiable interest in imaginary misfortunes and the fear of evil. Each adventure must be more dangerous than the last or more fearsome, and each rescue must be more strange and more happy.

The play explores a whole wonderful world, Antioch, Tarsus, Pentapolis, Tyre, so many great cities of the past, and it is full of kings and the daughters of kings with here and there plain people and here and there derelicts. But the chief interest of the play is not in the variety of the scene, although that provides the means of the play's development, but instead in the succession of one man's misfortunes and his final happiness. This various world and its fantastic actions all serve finally some interest for the audience in the progress of Pericles, and sooner or later the drama of adventure becomes a drama within a man and the resolution of the play is the resolution of a life.

The artifices of the play, the stock sophistications of the Greek romances, with the help of poetry lend something of the usual power of romances, suggesting the world of the East and the mysteries of strange oceans. The most markedly romantic devices—tournaments, shipwrecks, ministerial villains—create suspense at various times with their half-serious fear of evil, but other devices, closer to those of folklore, present more terrible images of evil, and the beginning situation of the play is one of these, the incident of a man who must solve a riddle to win a bride and by the same deed solve his own life. What is in itself a horrible enough circumstance, a man in the midst of the skeletons of those who have failed before him in this very trial, is made more terrible by the peculiar villainy of those whose riddle would deceive him, their incest destroying the value of what he sought and hoped to win. And in the end the play must resolve all the horrors, the real and the fantastic.

The initial adventure, the solving of the riddle, is, of course, the beginning of our interest in the action of the play, and this means at just our first interest in Pericles' success at evading the death Antiochus prepares for him now that his secret has escaped. But the presentation of Pericles' state of mind soon becomes a matter of still greater concern as we wonder about this young prince who has committed his hopes to the thought of a maiden entirely beautiful and who is now suddenly deprived of her. Most of the adventures that follow in his wanderings, in his flight from an assassin and then the strange happenings in distant ports, become increasingly absorbing but not because they reveal the skill and abilities of some Odysseus-like man escaping monsters. What leads us on is something about the peculiar consequence each adventure has for Pericles' soul, the loss of that promised happiness, and, temporarily at least, his kingdom; his winning a wife only to lose her and their daughter too, both supposedly by death; his falling into apathy; the question of the malignity of fortune and the remorselessness of the storms in the sea and the world. The interest that comes to govern us most is some suspense in the question of Pericles' ability to survive these evils and this suffering, and our interest in the sequence of adventures leads us always into thoughts about his sorrow. The end of the play is thus a most happily accepted resolution both of the story and of Pericles' despair, like a miracle and in fact a miracle; like a miracle in the bringing back of Thaisa and Marina from their supposed deaths; and in fact a miracle in Pericles' vision, when after Marina's song he hears the music of the spheres and is as it were himself restored to life.

—John Arthos, "*Pericles, Prince of Tyre:* A Study in the Dramatic Use of Romantic Narrative." *Shakespeare Quarterly* 4 (1953): pp. 257–259.

Plot Summary of
Cymbeline

Written sometime between 1608 and 1611 (probably concurrently with *The Winter's Tale*), the strongest evidence indicates that *Cymbeline* was first performed in 1611. Comprised of a series of interwoven stories, the sources for the play are principally Holinshed's *Chronicles,* Boccaccio's *Decameron,* and an anonymous play entitled *The Rare Triumphs of Love and Fortune.* Holinshed's *Chronicles* provide much of the play's pseudo-historical background.

Briefly stated, the "historical" framework for *Cymbeline* concerns a war between Britain and Rome, with Imogen the heir to the crown of a mythical ancient Britain and with the marital relationship between Imogen (sometimes written as Innogen) and Posthumus, which is broken up and eventually re-created, mirroring the collapse and restoration of relations between Britain and Rome.

Boccaccio's *Decameron,* a series of tales told by a group of traveling pilgrims, also had a strong influence on this play. Specifically, it is the ninth tale of *Decameron,* about Bernabo, a husband who maintains that he is "blessed with a wife who was possibly without equal in the whole of Italy . . . the ideal woman . . . the most chaste and honest" and the mockery of Ambrogiuolo (Shakespeare's Giacomo) asking whether the Emperor has granted Bernabo a special privilege in such as perfect wife. Bernabo's response to this jibe is to offer his own "head on the block" if Ambogiuolo is able to seduce his wife. In both Boccaccio and Shakespeare, the outcome of the wager does not end in its tragic potential, but instead in beauty and virtue preserved.

The last of the sources is the anonymous play, *The Rare Triumphs of Love and Fortune,* an old romantic drama performed at the Elizabethan court. The main action of *The Rare Triumphs* is framed by a dispute among the gods, presided over by Jupiter, the supreme god of the Roman state, as to whether Love (Venus) or Fortune has the greater power. The dispute ends with a reconciliation between the two contending parties. In this play, the two lovers who are used as experiments in Jupiter's game are the princess Fidelia (a name suggesting faith) and Hermione who (like Posthumus) is brought up in the court by Fidelia's father. In *The Rare Triumphs,* however, Hermione, is the son of Lord Bomelio, who was a victim of slander and therefore banished to a cave. When Hermione is in turn banished, he and the princess meet at Bomelio's cave. Though the young lovers are pursued by Fidelia's evil brother Armenio, Armenio is eventually struck dumb by the magic of Bomelio himself.

In **Act I** of Shakespeare's *Cymbeline,* two gentlemen present a problem in King Cymbeline's family that affects the entire realm. The king has several children from a previous marriage (his two sons, Guiderius and Arviragus, have been abducted), and remarried after the death of his first wife. The new Queen wanted to solidify her family's claim to the throne of Britain through the marriage of her son, Cloten, to Cymbeline's daughter, Imogen. However, against her father's wishes Imogen married her longtime childhood friend Posthumus, Cymbeline's adopted son. Cymbeline is enraged by this act of defiance; he imprisons Imogen and banishes Posthumus. The young couple make great protestations of their love for each other, as Posthumus promises that "I will remain / The loyal'st husband that e'er plight troth . . . I'll drink the words you send / Though ink be made of gall," before being separated by Cymbeline.

While living in exile in Italy with his friend Philario, Posthumus attends a party where he meets Iachimo and enters into a bet with him. This is the famous wager scene in which Posthumus, who has made great claims for the virtue of his new bride, is challenged by the boastful Iachimo, who predicts that he will seduce Imogen and thus invalidate Posthumus's faith in her fidelity. Posthumus accepts the challenge.

Later on in Act I, while Imogen is enduring a melancholic separation from her beloved Posthumus, the sly Iachimo is busy setting the stage for his intended seduction. He begins by having a letter delivered to the unsuspecting Imogen that informs her of Posthumus' infidelity, giving him the epithet of "the Briton Reveller." Iachimo, of course, does this in order to provide himself as the willing vehicle of sexual revenge on her unfaithful Posthumus. While observing her on the sidelines, he prays for the presumption to continue with this deception. "Boldness be my friend / Arm me audacity from head to foot."

But Imogen is only briefly deceived and quickly understands the game Iachimo is playing. Iachimo now has no other recourse but to admit that he was testing her virtue. He uses his rhetorical powers now to praise her equally trustworthy husband ("[b]lessèd live you long, / A lady to the worthiest sir that ever / Country called this") and takes his leave by asking her to care for a trunk of valuables, rare plates and jewels, which he and some other Romans intend as a present for the Emperor. Imogen agrees to watch over the trunk.

In the meantime, back in Cymbeline's court, the Queen seeks the help of a doctor, Cornelius, to bring her a box of poison. However, Cornelius is very suspicious ("I do know her spirit, / And will not trust one of her malice with / A drug of such damned nature"). Instead, in one of the many life-saving turns of the plot, the good doctor substitutes a "cordial," or magic potion, that will induce a deathlike sleep, but will happily cause the "victim" to awaken refreshed.

In **Act II,** when Imogen falls asleep, the relentless trickster Iachimo, who wants nothing more than to win his bet, emerges from the trunk, thoroughly enjoying the deception and reward to come. While she sleeps, Iachimo is able to make a thorough inspection of her physical appearance, memorizing such details as "a mole cinque-spotted" under her breast; these details, he believes, will convince Posthumus that a seduction did indeed take place. As further proof, Iachimo takes the bracelet Posthumus had given her and sets off for Italy to claim the prize from Posthumus. Indeed, Iachimo is so convincing that he causes Posthumus to proclaim the untrustworthiness of women. "For there's no motion / That tends to vice in man but I affirm / It is the woman's part."

In **Act III,** another display of Cymbeline's weakness takes place. Caius Lucius, the ambassador sent by Augustus Caesar, arrives at the British Court to demand the tribute that Cymbeline's uncle had promised to Julius Caesar, but before the King can reply, the Queen and Cloten absolutely and rudely refuse to comply. Later on in this same act, Cymbeline realizes that the Queen's belligerence will invoke war with Caesar. The next scene at court involves Posthumus's servant, Pisanio, who receives a letter commanding him to kill Imogen for her act of betrayal. Pisanio, however, cannot believe Imogen guilty of any transgression, and feels he can not harm her. Further on, Pisanio offers to say that he killed Imogen in order to placate the raging Posthumus, but Imogen refuses the ruse because of her fear that she will now have to marry Cloten when the rift with Posthumus becomes known. Pisanio then suggests that Imogen flee the court, disguised in male clothing, with the aid of a magic potion that will cure everything. She could, he suggests, embark upon a mission to serve the noble Lucius who is coming their way. Imogen, however, is determined to meet Posthumus. When Cloten finds out, he is determined to thwart her plans by dressing in Posthumus' clothing.

While all these troubles and machinations are taking shape at court, there is an intervening scene that shifts our focus to Wales, where Belarius, another exiled lord, has been living and rearing Cymbeline's two long-lost sons. Together, they all live in a very unpretentious rural retreat, where all must pitch in and do their part. Eventually, Imogen meets up with the two sons at the cave home of Belarius, where she immediately intuits their inherent royalty, proclaiming them "[g]reat men / That had a court no bigger than this cave."

In **Act IV,** Cloten raves to himself that despite all his efforts Imogen still prefers Posthumus, and claims that he will cut off his rival's head. Cloten, however, gets his just reward when Guiderius, whom Cloten has insulted, decapitates this despicable rogue. And, at the same time, Imogen, while lying sick in the cave, takes the magic "cordial" Pisanio had previously given her, and falls into a very deep sleep. Believing she is dead, Belarius and "his two sons" perform the rituals of mourning, only to have her awaken to the decapitated head of Cloten. She mistakes him for Posthumus, because he is disguised in Posthumus' clothes. Imogen is grief-stricken and outraged against both Pisanio and Cloten, holding them responsible for the bloody deed.

In **Act V,** Posthumus, who has been supplied with "proof" of Imogen's infidelity in the form of a bloody cloth, now regrets his rage. "So I'll fight / Against the part I come with; so I'll die / For thee, O Imogen, even for whom my life is every breath a death." In a world of many disguises, Posthumus now decides to don the clothes of a peasant and join the war against the Romans, who he has been accompanying. Meanwhile, Cymbeline is captured and then released by Belarius and his two "lost" sons. Posthumus then offers himself to the British as a prisoner, while praising the heroism of those responsible for Cymbeline's rescue. Posthumus's contribution is not lost when Cymbeline remembers the "poor soldier" who joined them in battle. We also learn from the good doctor, Cornelius, that the queen has died, "[w]ith horror, madly dying, like her life / Which being cruel to the world, concluded / Most cruel to herself." While all of this is happening, Posthumus, in his prison cell, dreams of his lost family, who pray to Jupiter for his sake.

In the end, all the diverse plots are brought together. Imogen is re-united with Posthumus, and she exacts an admission of guilt from Iachimo ("I am down again, / But now my heavy conscience sinks my knee"). Cymbeline's "lost" sons celebrate that their sister is indeed alive. Finally, the young lovers are reinstated into the royal court, and all is made right as Cymbeline proclaims: "See, / Posthumus anchors upon Imogen, / And she, like harmless lightning, throws her eye / On him, her brothers, me, her master, hitting / Each object with a joy." And so the play ends with the state restored to complete harmony and Cymbeline promising to pay the tribute he owes. ❀

List of Characters in
Cymbeline

Cymbeline, King of Britain, is a monarch who is beset by serious domestic and political crises and who demonstrates his own weak character in succumbing to his new Queen. Cymbeline is also facing political problems with Rome, when an ambassador sent by Augustus Caesar, arrives at the British Court to demand the tribute that Cymbeline's uncle had promised to Julius Caesar, but never paid.

The Queen is Cymbeline's second wife. She immediately reveals her thirst for power in seeking to assure that her son, Cloten, will marry Cymbeline's daughter from his previous marriage and thereby secure the throne.

Imogen is Cymbeline's daughter by a former queen. When she marries Posthumus, Cymbeline's son of a prior marriage, she enrages the king and is imprisoned, thereby separating the two lovers. A very idealized woman symbolic of chastity and fidelity. Although Giacomo attempts to provoke her into seek a jealous revenge against her husband, Imogen is only briefly deceived and quickly understands the game Giacomo is playing. After Cloten is beheaded, Imogen briefly mistakes his head as belonging to her beloved Posthumus because Cloten, who will go to any extreme to win, is dressed in Posthumus' clothing.

Posthumus Leontus is Imogen's husband and Cymbeline's adopted son. Upon learning of his marriage to Imogen, Cymbeline banishes Posthumus. While in exile in in Italy with his friend **Philario,** Posthumus meets Giacomo and enters into a wager with him as to the unfailing virtue of his new bride.

A servant to Posthumus, **Pisanio** receives a letter directing him to kill Imogen for her infidelity. However, he suggests that she flee the court disguised in male clothing.

Iachimo is a mischievous rogue full of self-importance. Once he persuades Posthumus to enter into the wager, Iachimo busies himself plotting his intended seduction of the unsuspecting Imogen, and begins by having a letter delivered to her which falsely accuses Posthumus' of being unfaithful while he is living in exile.

Cloten is the Queen's son by a former marriage. He is stupid, hostile, and given to swearing. When Cloten finds out that Posthumus and

Imogen plan to meet, he is determined to thwart her plans by dressing in Posthumus' clothing. Cloten, however, gets his just reward when Guiderius, whom Cloten has insulted, decapitates this despicable rogue.

Belarius is a banished lord living in Wales under the name Morgan. While in exile, Belarious has been living and rearing Cymbeline's two long-lost sons. Together, they all live in a very unpretentious rural retreat.

Guiderius and **Arviragus** are Cymbeline's sons, disguised under the names Polydore and Cadwal, respectively. Guiderius is the one who cuts off Cloten's head as revenge for Cloten having insulted him. ❀

Critical Views on
Cymbeline

PEGGY MUÑOZ SIMONDS ON THE EAGLE'S MYTHIC
MEANINGS

[Peggy Muñoz Simonds is the author of *Myth, Emblem, and
Music in Shakespeare's Cymbeline* (1992). In the excerpt below, she discusses the traditional mythic meanings of the eagle in the Renaissance and its application to Posthumus'
status.]

Many students of *Cymbeline* have wondered why Posthumus is also
compared to an eagle by Imogen, who proudly informs her father, "I
chose an eagle, / And did avoid a puttock" (1.2.70–71). The three traditional meanings of the eagle during the Renaissance were keen vision, royalty, and the ability to gaze directly into the sun. When we
consider each of these in turn, we soon realize that Posthumus has
none of these qualities.

First, the eagle was known as a bird with exceptionally keen vision.
According to Rowland,

> In the [iconographic] presentation of the Five Senses, the eagle was the
> attribute of Sight. Isidore had claimed that even the eagle's name *aquila*
> derived from *acumine,* the acuteness of its eyes, and as late as 1652
> Bernini chose an eagle flying towards the sun as the frontispiece for a
> scientific work on optics.

In 1582, Stephan Batman reminded his Elizabethan readers that "ye
eagle is called Aquila, and hath that name of sharpnesse of eien, as
Isidor sayth." Yet Shakespeare's Posthumus sees very little of the reality underlying appearances throughout most of the play. He is naively
willing to believe calumny against his bride; he fails to see through the
bloody cloth that serves as a false token of her death; and in the last
scene of *Cymbeline,* he still does not recognize Imogen disguised as the
page Fidele and roughly knocks her down for interrupting his histri-
onic expressions of grief.

Second, the eagle was widely considered to be the bird of royalty,
and Shakespeare had made previous use of it as a regal symbol in

3 Henry VI: "Nay, if thou be that princely eagle's bird, / Show thy descent by gazing 'gainst the sun" (3.2.1). Posthumus, however, is not royal by birth, although he assumes royalty through his marriage to Imogen and is then considered "poison" to the blood of the king. Nor does the hero at first display the royal qualities of "fearlessness, intrepidity, and magnanimity" usually associated with the eagle, if we judge him by his actions rather than by what others say of him. Indeed, James Siemon correctly observes that "the judgment of Posthumus' worth in I, i, is at odds with much of the play's action." Actors struggling to prepare the role of Posthumus have been especially puzzled by this rather foolish "eagle." Roger Rees of the Royal Shakespeare Company reports, for example, that finally "I realized that poor Posthumus had so much to live up to that he had to take a tumble, sooner or later. Being famous at too early an age is a gift that only the most resilient prodigy can handle. . . . [But then] I started to get a sense of the ridiculous, which leads to fondness and eventual redemption in characters so stiff." However, to be amusing, the eagle must be seen as molting or in some way vulnerable. 〈 . . . 〉

Third, the Renaissance believed that the eagle could gaze directly into the sun. Rudolf Wittkower points out that this peculiar ability of the eagle often had an amorous meaning in that "The beloved is the sun at which the lover alone is allowed to look." However, at Philario's house in Rome, the Frenchman does not seem very impressed by Posthumus as an ideal Neoplatonic lover in competition with the French courtiers: "I have seen him in France; we had very many / There could behold the sun with as firm eyes as he" (1.5.10–11). At least he does admit that Posthumus can gaze directly at the sun in true eagle fashion. Nonetheless, Posthumus soon completely fails on the test of his own proclaimed faithfulness in love when he makes a wager on his bride's chastity and thereby permits Iachimo to gaze upon Imogen's naked beauty while she sleeps. Significantly, the men who behave this way in Shakespeare's principal sources for the wager story, *The Decameron* and *Frederyke of Jennen,* are husbands from the merchant class rather than the nobility and are plainly more interested in the money they hope to win from the wager than in the honor of their wives. More importantly, neither of them is ever compared to an eagle.

But there was a widely known myth about the eagle, which Shakespeare and his Renaissance audience knew and which might have allowed the audience to accept Posthumus as legitimately analogous to the eagle, despite his obvious failings. This was an early Christian story of the eagle written down by Physiologus in Greek, possibly as early as the second century A.D., and regularly included, often with further commentaries, in the bestiaries of the Middle Ages. It reappeared as a commonplace in Renaissance emblem books and was again recounted in the mythological sections of early attempts at scientific ornithology, such as the exhaustive 1599 Latin encyclopedia on birds by Aldrovandi. The myth describes three separate events in the life of the eagle, all of which were part of an attempt by Physiologus to explain David's promise in Psalm 103 that "Your youth will be renewed like the eagle's" and to relate the three motifs symbolically to the spiritual fall, reform, and regeneration of humanity. Essentially it is the story of a religious conversion, an event that Shakespeare actually dramatizes in act 5, scene 4 of *Cymbeline.* Moreover, the general pattern of decline into sin, the fall, and the ultimate renewal described in this eagle myth is roughly analogous to the pattern of Posthumus's life in the play. He betrays Imogen through the sin of pride when he boasts of her chastity in Rome; he falls into the temptation of gaining forbidden knowledge about her chastity from Iachimo; and he later renews himself through humble penitance and a symbolic change of clothing, or the molting of his fancy Roman feathers.

—Peggy Muñoz Simonds, *Myth, Emblem, and Music in Shakespeare's Cymbeline* (Newark: University of Delaware Press, 1992): pp. 213–215.

⊗

ROGER WARREN ON IMOGEN'S CHASTITY

[Roger Warren is the author of *Staging Shakespeare's Late Plays* (1990). In the excerpt below from his introduction to *Cymbeline,* Warren discusses the folkloric and literary origins of the wager on Imogen's chastity.]

The story of the wager on Innogen's chastity has its origins in folklore. Myths and folk-tales always embody some deep-rooted human emotion, what Stephen Orgel calls 'the terrifying truths of the inner life'; and this one focuses on the psychological insecurity inherent in any intimate relationship, a topic searchingly explored elsewhere in Shakespeare's work and summarized in the trenchant final line of Sonnet 92: 'Thou mayst be false, and yet I know it not.' The folk-tale of the husband who wagers on his wife's chastity in fact expresses less the confidence which the husband claims he feels than his lack of trust in his wife: she is being put to the test. Although at the start of *Cymbeline* the First Gentleman offers an ideal image of Posthumus as a heroic paragon (I.I.17–24), the process of the wager soon begins to modify that image. 'It might', says R. A. Foakes, 'be thought a hollow confidence in [Innogen] that drives Posthumus to brag so much that she is "more fair, virtuous, wise, chaste, constant, qualified, and less attemptable" than the rarest ladies of France'. There is something, if not exactly sordid, at least spiritually mean, in making a bet on your wife's purity; this is emphasized when the Frenchman points out that Posthumus got himself into trouble by making such claims before (I.4.32–58), and it is reinforced by Shakespeare's principal source for the wager story.

Although this story was in such wide currency as a folk-tale, the immediate impulse for Shakespeare was unquestionably the ninth tale of the second day of Boccaccio's *Decameron*. No English translation earlier than 1620 has survived, although since the printer of that translation pointed out that many of the stories 'have long since been published before', it is possible that Shakespeare knew a translation that has not survived. Otherwise, he must have read it in Italian or in one of the numerous sixteenth-century French translations of the *Decameron,* for simply to read straight through Boccaccio's story reveals its illuminating closeness to *Cymbeline* not merely in events, but more crucially in tone and attitude. Like Posthumus, Bernabò, the husband in the *Decameron,* maintains that he is 'blessed with a wife who was possibly without equal in the whole of Italy, . . . endowed with all the qualities of the ideal woman, . . . the most chaste and honest woman to be found anywhere on earth'. This provokes the mockery of Ambrogiuolo, the equivalent of Shakespeare's Giacomo, who asks whether the Emperor had granted him the privilege of such a perfect wife: 'Faintly annoyed, Bernabò replied that this favour had been conceded to him, not by the Emperor, but by God, who was a little more powerful'. This clearly suggested both Posthumus' claim that Innogen is 'only the gift of the gods' and Giacomo's ironic response 'Which the gods have given you?" (I.4.81–2); but perhaps the close relationship with Boccaccio emerges still more clearly in the way that Shakespeare adopts, for Giacomo particularly, the bantering tone of passages that he does not in fact use; for example, Bernabò, proposing the wager, extravagantly offers, 'in order to convince you of my lady's integrity, to place my head on the block' if Ambrogiuolo succeeds in seducing his wife; Ambrogiuolo takes the wind out of Bernabò's sails, as Giacomo often does to Posthumus' (I.4.84–5, 129–32; 2.4.95–8, 105), by replying: 'I wouldn't know what to do with your head, if I were to win. But if you really want to see proof of what I have been saying, you can put up five thousand florins of your own, which is less than you'd pay for a new head, against my thousand.' When Boccaccio says that by the end of their dispute 'the passions of the two men were so strongly aroused that, contrary to the wishes of the others, they drew up a form of contract . . . which was binding on both parties', he might be summarizing the development of Shakespeare's scene. Posthumus' bragging about Innogen needles Giacomo, who is specific about his motivation: 'I make my wager rather against your confidence than her reputation' (I.4.106–7); and in the process he releases Posthumus' touchiness and inner insecurity about his wife's sexuality. Boccaccio provides an interesting perspective on the behavior of both Bernabò and Posthumus when he has the narrator of the following story mock the 'foolishness of such people as Bernabò'. The model for Posthumus, then, is a stupid man who doesn't trust his wife and has a lot to learn.

—Roger Warren, Introduction to *Cymbeline*, by William Shakespeare (Oxford: Clarendon Press, 1998): pp. 26–28.

PETER ALEXANDER ON IMOGEN'S VOICE

[Peter Alexander has written extensively on Shakespeare. His books include *Hamlet: Father and Son* (1963), *Alexander's Introductions to Shakespeare* (1964), and *Shakespeare's Life and Art* (1967). In the following excerpt, Alexander discusses the captivating and romantic atmosphere of *Cymbeline* and the dramatic expression of that setting which is brought about through Imogen's voice.]

The story of Cymbeline Shakespeare found in Holinshed's romantic histories of the early British kings and their dealings with the Romans. In the final battle-piece, he adapted the same historian's account of how a Scotsman and his two sons decided a battle against the Danes by their unexpected and resolute intervention. To this Shakespeare added an Italianate intrigue from the *Decameron* (II, 9), which he consulted in the original, as the conclusion of Boccaccio's story, turned to comic use in *The Winter's Tale,* does not appear in *Frederick of Jennen,* the only known available version in English.

Judged from the historical or realistic standpoint the result merits Johnson's censure:

> To remark the folly of the fiction, the absurdity of the conduct, the confusion of the names and manners of different times, and the impossibility of the events in any system of life, were to waste criticism upon unresisting imbecility, upon faults too evident for detection, and too gross for aggravation.

But as Shakespeare was not writing a history but a play, the only relevant question is how all this affects the imagination. And the prevalence of the fabulous over the real in the Romances, a characteristic mark, according to Longinus, of the work of a great genius that has past its intensest phase, is felt to correspond to a state of mind in Shakespeare that has far-reaching parallels in the development of other great artists.

What gives unity to Shakespeare's last works is the atmosphere in which he has steeped them. Turner at the end painted light, and his final inspirations rise like some miraculous dome on the sure foundations of his earlier science. Shakespeare became preoccupied with a comparable radiance in the inner world of drama. Lytton Strachey talks of his style as now everything, as one might talk of Turner's or Rembrandt's colour being everything in their final masterpieces. But no one supposes that this is a sign of boredom in the painters, or anything but a transformation and intensification of certain life-long interests.

The golden haze of *Cymbeline* naturally captivated such an artist as Tennyson, but it was still his favorite play when he knew he had done with art. For though Shakespeare in the setting of his days seems like the poet gazing westward in the afterglow, his thoughts

> sunk far
> Leagues beyond the sunset bar,

though his longings are like Imogen's 'beyond beyond,' he looks forward to the gulfs of evening over no strand forlorn. It is as if the human voice to which he had been so responsive still sounded in his ears, making what was already unearthly into 'a kind of heavenly destiny.' For the Romances give sustained and dramatic expression to the vision that finds momentary expression in the lines,

> and while my eye
> Was fixed upon the glowing Sky,
> The echo of the voice enwrought
> A human sweetness with the thought
> Of travelling through the world that lay
> Before me in my endless way.

It is, of course, the voice of Imogen that gives its meaning to this play, as it is the voices of Hamlet and Lear that give significance to their tragedies.

Imogen, the last of Shakespeare's long line of heroines who have to masquerade as boys, is, though a married woman, in some ways the most romantic of them all. On this point Hazlitt, as strong an admirer of the play as Tennyson, in his own different way, wrote:

> No one ever hit the true perfection of the female character, the sense of weakness leaning on the strength of its affections for support, so well as Shakespeare—no one else ever so well painted natural tenderness free from affection and disguise—no one else ever so well showed how delicacy and timidity, when driven to extremity, grow romantic and extravagant; for the romance of his heroines (in which they abound) is only an excess of the habitual prejudices of their sex, scrupulous of being false to their vows, truant to their affections and taught by the force of feeling when to forgo the forms of propriety for the essence of it.

Hers is the heavenly alchemy that gilds to some tint of brightness even the basest characters in the story. 'I am distressed in the *Cymbeline*,' wrote Bridges, 'by the contact of Iachimo with Imogen, and its great unpleasantness is evidently due to the exquisite beauty of Shakespeare's creation.' But part of that beauty had escaped us but for the subtle Italian's contribution to its sum. Iachimo no less than Cloten or the simple mountaineers is a mirror to reflect the heroine. Each shows an image in accord with its quality and kind. 'How angel-like he sings,' says the enthusiastic Arviragus of the disguised Imogen, and his older and more prosaic brother adds, 'But his neat cookery.' The scenes between Imogen and Iachimo are an essential part of the portrait, and

Iachimo's soliloquy in her bedchamber one of the triumphs of the play. And without his gross talk with Posthumus, and the outspoken fury to which this drives his dupe, how much reality and life would be wanting in this portrait?

Though Shakespeare may have been quite indifferent to historic probability he was, as Hazlitt noted, careful to adapt his material for the stage:

> The last act is crowded with decisive events brought about by natural and striking means. . . . The fate of almost every person in the drama is made to depend on the solution of a single circumstance— the answer of Iachimo to a question of Imogen respecting the obtaining of the ring from Posthumus.

When Shakespeare comes to what demands careful treatment he can still show his old craft.

—Peter Alexander, *Shakespeare's Life and Art* (New York: New York University Press, 1967): pp. 206–209.

John Philip Brockbank on Shakespeare's Sources

[John Philip Brockbank has edited an edition of Ben Jonson's *Volpone* (1968) and *Approaches to Marvell: The York Tercentenary Lectures* (1978). In the excerpt below, Brockbank focuses on Shakespeare's sources and his creative use of fiction as a way of expressing certain historical truths.]

The sources of *Cymbeline* are sufficiently known. What now are we to do with them? Source-hunting offers its own satisfactions and it is an acceptable mode of conspicuous leisure, but it should be possible still to bring it to bear more closely on the problems of literary criticism. Its bearing, however, may differ from play to play. It is salutatory, for instance, to recognize that striking debt owed by *The Tempest* to travel literature. ⟨ . . . ⟩

Cymbeline is a different problem. It is not so self-evident a masterpiece. There is the common passage and there is the strain of rareness. The sources and analogues could be used to explain away whatever fails to make an immediate, effacing impression. But they have too, I think, a more positive value. They can show that many of the play's uniquely impressive effects could have been won only out of that specific area of convention that Shakespeare chose to explore. Within this area we can distinguish something like a dramatic genre, and as a label we might take Polonius' infelicity 'historical-pastoral' or, in deference to received opinion, 'historical romance'. Such labels are useful because they tell us what sort of conventions to look out for, although each play is apt to define its own area, make its own map. My emphasis will be on the 'historical', for there is, I think, a way of reading the sources which lends support to Wilson Knight's claim that *Cymbeline* is to be regarded "mainly as an historical play". Criticism may fault his quite remarkable 'interpretation' for trying to evoke a maximum pregnancy from conventions that are insufficiently transmuted from their chronicle and theatrical analogues; but it cannot fault him for recognizing that the fictions of *Cymbeline,* while owing nothing to the factual disciplines commonly called 'historical', seek nevertheless to express certain truths about the processes which have shaped the past of Britain. I shall argue that even the 'romantic significance' of the play is worth mastering, and that we can best master it by way of the chronicle sources.

To initiate the appropriate dialogue between the play and its sources, we might say that *Cymbeline* is about a golden world delivered from a brazen by the agency of a miraculous providence. That archaic formulation would not have startled Shakespeare's contemporaries, and it might equally preface a discussion of the play's alleged transcendent meaning or of its manifest indebtedness to convention. I mean to use it first, however, as a clue to track Shakespeare's reading through the labyrinth of Holinshed.

Holinshed's brief notice of the reign of Kymbeline reads like an old tale, and Shakespeare clearly felt no obligation to treat it as fact. He distinguished firmly between the Tudor material, whose documentary force he retained in the earlier histories, and the Brutan, with which he took the fullest liberties in *Lear* and *Cymbeline.*

There is, however, no obvious reason why he should have turned his attention unhesitatingly to Kymbeline, and since the names of the characters are scattered over a wide span of pages in the second edition of Holinshed, we may be confident that he was widely read in the Brutan phase of the history, that he began at the beginning, and that he read it quite early, culling the name "Iago" in its course. We may indeed regard *Cymbeline* and *Henry VIII* as the last fruits of the Brutan and Tudor chronicles in Shakespeare's dramatic art. They might be presented as complemental plays—a fantastical history and a historical fantasy, but the exercise would be premature without some excursion into the reading behind *Cymbeline*.

The First Chapter of the *Second Booke of the Historie of England* did most, I think, to determine the form and tenor of the play. It tells of the descent and early life of Brute, and includes this passage:

> To this opinion Giouan Villani a Florentine in his vniuersall historie, speaking of Aeneas and his ofspring kings in Italie, seemeth to agree, where he saith: "Silius (the sonne of Aeneas by his wife Lauinia) fell in loue with a neece of his mother Lauinia, and by hir had a sonne, of whom she died in trauell, and therefore was called Brutus, who after as he grew in some stature, and hunting in a forrest slue his father vnawares, and therevpon for feare of his grandfather Siluius Posthumus he fled the countrie, and with a retinue of such as followed him, passing through diuers seas, until at length he arriued in the Ile of Britaine." ⟨ . . . ⟩
>
> His grandfather (whether the same was Posthumus, or his elder brother) hearing of this great misfortune that had happened to his sonne Siluius, liued not long after, but died for verie greefe and sorow (as is supposed) which he conceiued thereof. And the yoong gentleman, immediatlie after he had slaine his father (in manner before alledged) was banished his countrie, and therevpon got him into Grecia, where trauelling the countrie, he lighted by chance among some of the Troian ofspring, and associating himselfe with them, grew by meanes of the lineage (whereof he was descended) in proces of time into great reputation among them: chieflie by reason there were yet diuers of the Troian race, and that of great authoritie in that countrie.

There is little here that would be admitted as a 'source' by the criteria of Boswell-Stone, but Shakespeare may well have recognized an opportunity to deploy the conventions of romance in a play made from one or other of the Brutan legends. His story of the lost princes as it has finally reached us is an invention not owed to, but consonant with the strange adventures of Brute. And *Cymbeline* touches, in a different order and to changed effect, the motifs of mysterious descent, hunting, murder (a boy killing a prince), banishment, and chance (or providential) encounter with offspring of the same lineage. There is a kind of obligation here, and in his choice of the names Posthumus and Innogen (the wife of Brute) Shakespeare seems to offer a playful salute of acknowledgement.

The second chapter offers another piece of ready-made theatrical apparatus. Brute and Innogen "arrive in Leogitia" and "aske counsell of an oracle where they shall inhabit". Brute kneels, "holding in his right hand a boll prepared for sacrifice full of wine, and the bloude of a white hinde", and after he has done his "praier and ceremonie . . . according to the pagane rite and custome", he falls asleep. The goddess Diana speaks Latin verses (which the chronicle translates) sending him to an isle "farre by-west beyond the Gallike land". "After he awaked out of sleepe", the chronicle goes on, "and had called his dreame to remembrance, he first doubted whether it were a verie dreame, or a true vision, the goddess hauing spoken to him with liuelie voice". Once again, the vision is not a source but an occasion. It may have licensed the vision of Posthumus—a stage theophany in a play which, like the myth, is concerned with the ancestral virtue and destiny of Britain. Shakespeare drew of course on his own experience of the theatre and perhaps on a memory of *The Rare Triumphs* for the specific form of the theophany, but whether by chance or design the verse form is oddly consonant with the chronicle.

—John Philip Brockbank, "History and Histrionics in *Cymbeline*." *Shakespeare Survey* 11 (1958): pp. 42–44.

⊕

Michael Taylor on the Grotesque in Imogen's Dream

[In the excerpt below, Taylor discusses the vehicle of the grotesque in Imogen's death-like dream as a way of diminishing malicious energy, which later enables her to enter into a civilized Roman world.]

The most astonishing scene in *Cymbeline* unnerves us with the grotesque spectacle of its heroine waking up in a pastoral setting from a death-like sleep (induced by Dr Cornelius' box of drugs) to the sight of what appears to be her decapitated husband sprawled alongside her. *Et in Arcadia ego*, with a vengeance! Until this rude awakening, Imogen had imagined herself to be safe in her pastoral sanctuary, far from the corruption of Cymbeline's court, secure in the immediate and excessive affection displayed for her by Arviragus and Guiderius who, despite her male disguise, and despite the fact that they have never met her before, have instinctively and conventionally responded to the ties of blood between them. Horrified now by this change in her situation, Imogen at first concludes that she must be dreaming:

> I hope I dream,
> For so I thought I was a cave-keeper
> And cook to honest creatures.
> (4.5.297–9)

The desired diminution of her status from princess to pastoral skivvy has become mysteriously transformed into a nightmare degradation in which the honest creatures of her waking hours have vanished, leaving behind in their place a headless changeling whose reality can be only fleetingly doubted in those blurred moments 'twixt sleep and wake.

Imogen's enumeration of Posthumus' Herculean parts as she then inches her way up to the corpse's headlessness has shaken many critics; as Bernard Harris observes, the whole scene has a 'comic menace and near-demented ingenuity'. 'Dramatically inexcusable' for Harley Granville-Barker, Imogen's final confrontation with Cloten is a notoriously difficult one to bring off in the theatre without arousing a defensive risibility in an audience alarmed by the extent to which Shakespeare has already subjected his heroine to the unspeakable. ⟨ . . . ⟩

Shakespeare seems determined to invest Cloten's remains with a more remarkable potency than their owner ever managed when alive, while still maintaining his essential absurdity even when the cause of it has been so unceremoniously removed. Brainless while alive, Cloten's fate is grim poetic justice: his headless carcass a bizarre rebus for the conduct of his life. In death, his absurdity is infectious. In all the previous confrontations between Cloten and Imogen, Cloten has come halting off, his precarious intellect no match for Imogen's sarcastic tongue and unshakeable dignity; now, in mute triumph, his body, about which he had been so absurdly arrogant (that 'arrogant piece of flesh' (4.2.127) as Guiderius describes him), raises up a storm of emotion in Imogen's breast. The fact that she believes the body to belong to Posthumus makes the experience even more damaging to her dignity, especially when, in an excess of grief, she throws herself upon it in an action ironically—dementedly—almost farcically—precipitated by the name of the person (did she but know it) with whose blood she now daubs herself:

This is Pisanio's deed, and Cloten. O,
Give colour to my pale cheek with thy blood,
That we the horrider may seem to those
Which chance to find us. O my lord, my lord!
(4.2.329–32) ⟨ ... ⟩

While it may be true (as so many critics insist) that there has been something of an 'uneasy conflation' of history and romance in *Cymbeline*, or that the play as a whole fails to come together entirely satisfactorily, it is demonstrably true that in the story of Imogen, Iachimo, and Posthumus Shakespeare achieves a potent coherence in which the violation of Imogen's dream of pastoral innocence has an important role to play, as it also has in the play's action as a whole, making it one of those events of special significance in a work of art around which interpretation invariably clusters. After some forty lines or so of wild address over the decapitated body, Imogen falls into an exhausted sleep from which she awakes to another, more promising reality as attendant on her civilized Roman master, Caius Lucius. After Imogen's grotesque experience, malicious energy in the play as a whole flags— the scenes which follow act 4, scene 2 record a progressive amelioration: in act 4, scene 3, news of the Queen's fatal illness (we never see her again); in act 5, scene 1, Posthumus' repentance even before he knows Imogen to be guiltless; in act 5, scene 2, Iachimo's similar repentance following his defeat in battle by the disguised Posthumus; in the play's last three scenes, the military triumph of the Britons over the Romans, Posthumus' vision of Jupiter, Cymbeline's refreshed state of mind and his voluntary return to the *pax romana*.

In structural and emotional terms Imogen's degradation in act 4, scene 2 marks a watershed in the play's action; after it, with almost every wink of the eye some new grace will be born. Pivotally placed, Imogen's experience captures much of the play's accumulated significance, and the greater the interpretive burden the more daring Shakespeare's choice of the grotesque as an appropriate vehicle for this climax to the play's pastoral activity, in which an original dream of innocence—Imogen's—expressed in explicitly pastoral terms, undergoes such a savage assault.

—Michael Taylor, "The Pastoral Reckoning in 'Cymbeline.'" *Shakespeare Survey* 36 (1983): pp. 97–98.

❀

ARTHUR C. KIRSCH ON SHAKESPEARE'S "SELF-CONSCIOUSNESS"

[Arthur C. Kirsch is the author of *Shakespeare and the Experience of Love* (1981) and *Jacobean Dramatic Perspectives* (1972). In the excerpt below, Kirsch discusses the concept of "self-consciousness" for Shakespeare and his contemporaries.]

In 1608 the King's Men, of which Shakespeare was a principal shareholder, and for which he was the principal dramatist, acquired the Blackfriars Theater. *Cymbeline, The Winter's Tale* and *The Tempest* were probably performed there, as well as at the Globe, and the presumption is that at the very least Shakespeare wrote the plays so that they would please both audiences and be suitable to the conditions of both theaters. It is even possible, despite *Pericles,* which antedates the move to Blackfriars and seems designed for the public theater, that in *Cymbeline* Shakespeare was thinking primarily of the dramatic possibilities of the Blackfriars. It is no doubt a species of folly peculiar to theater historians to assume that once you explain the conditions of performance and the class of audience you explain the play, but it is surely just as foolish to assume that these things do not count at all, especially since there is so much evidence in Shakespeare's case not only that he was thoroughly professional, but that he was profoundly stirred by the idea and conventions of the theater itself.

The private playhouses had developed a distinctive idea of theater by the time Shakespeare became associated with Blackfriars, with a dramaturgy which was recognizably different from that of the Globe. Unfortunately most studies of coterie drama have so exaggerated the differences and so confused dramaturgy with morality that it has been very difficult to have a clear idea either of the nature of this drama or its possible effects upon the public theater. There has been, for example, no systematic study of the effect of conditions at Blackfriars upon the dramatic assumptions and structure of plays performed there, although there are studies of the theater itself and of the boy companies. There have been illuminating studies, however, of individual coterie dramatists, including Beaumont and Fletcher, and it is through Beaumont and Fletcher that the idea of theater which may have stimulated Shakespeare in *Cymbeline* and the later plays may best be formulated. ⟨ . . . ⟩

The most distinguishing feature of this dramaturgy is its deliberate self-consciousness. Beaumont and Fletcher's plays, like all plays, are designed to move an audience, but unlike plays at the Globe their effect depends upon the audience's consciousness of the means by which it is moved. No matter how many surprises they pull out of the plot, no matter how passionate their characters or intriguing their action, the play all the while calls attention to itself as a dramatic fiction. In part this is a natural consequence of the tragicomic pattern as Fletcher himself defined it in the preface to *The Faithful Shepherdess:* "A tragicomedie is not so called in respect of mirth and killing, but in respect it wants deaths, which is enough to make it no tragedy, yet brings some near it, which is enough to make it no comedy. . . . " Such a dramatic formulation leads necessarily, as Granville-Barker remarks of *Cymbeline,* to an "art that rather displays art than conceals it." In Beaumont and Fletcher this display is manifested in a pervasive emphasis upon the pattern and peripeties of the action rather than upon a continuous (and engaging) story dramatizing a theme, and in a conception of characterization which is discontinuous and deliberately indecorous. Their plays also place great stress upon what Dryden was later to call "argumentation and discourse," scene after scene of declamatory displays of passion and passionate reasoning. All of it adds up to a drama which is insistently and consciously theatrical in a manner somewhat like opera. James Shirley, in his preface to the 1647 Beaumont and Fletcher folio, described its effect very lucidly: "You may here find passions raised to that excellent pitch and by such insinuating degrees that you shall not chuse but consent, & go along with them, finding your self at last grown insensibly the very same person you read, and then stand admiring the subtile Trackes of your engagement." ⟨ . . . ⟩

A self-conscious dramaturgy—including discontinuous action emphasizing scenes rather than plot, and exaggerated characters manipulated for debate and passionate declamations—seems to have been a common denominator of many if not most plays written for the private theater. Moreover, this dramaturgy was not simply a result of the development of satirical comedy, for satirical comedy itself may be considered an early symptom of the larger movement in the English theater from the platform to the picture frame stage. There is a pervasive emphasis in satirical comedy upon parody, of traditional theatrical conventions as well as of traditional ideas, and such dramatists as Jonson and Beaumont and Fletcher are patronizing about precisely the public theater conventions which, like those of the modern movie, require the audience's uncritical involvement in a panoramic, continuous story. But in any case, it is demonstrable that a calculated self-consciousness was characteristic of many plays written for the private theater in the early seventeenth century and provided a new idea of tragicomic theater which subsequent dramatists could exploit, including those, like Shakespeare, whose earlier experience had been primarily in the public theater.

There are indications that this whole dramaturgical movement in the private theater was in fact suggestive to Shakespeare in his last plays. *Cymbeline* is the least harmonious of these plays, but perhaps because Shakespeare's genius is less distractingly present, the play also provides the clearest and strongest evidence of the ways in which the techniques and dramatic implications of coterie drama may have affected him. The salient fact about *Cymbeline*, to begin with, is that it is resistant to any coherent interpretation. The action moves freely through a kaleidoscope of milieux: a primitive British court, a Machiavellian Italy, a Roman Italy, a pastoral cave. Its hero is at best only half-admirable: in the beginning he loves Imogen and values her as "the gift of the gods" (I, v, 88); after Iachimo's deception he orders her death. Its principal villain is similarly only half-sinister: at possibly his most evil moment, when he is trying to seduce Imogen, Iachimo becomes so intoxicated with his own verbal extravagance that he subverts his own intentions. Cloten, a lesser villain to begin with, is also a clownish boor, as Shakespeare takes pains to establish in the scene with the Second Lord (I, iii); the Queen is never more than a cardboard figure; and Cymbeline is not much more than a dupe. Imogen, the principal and unifying figure of interest in the play, is less equivocally portrayed, since in herself she is consistent enough. But on the other hand the play deals with her very strangely. In a scene that is studiously prepared for, the *scène à faire* of the play, she awakens by the headless body of Cloten, who is dressed in Posthumus' garments, and mistaking him for her husband she sings "an aria of agony." It is a moving and convincing one, but we cannot help being conscious at the same time, as Granville-Barker remarks, that "it is a fraud on Imogen; and we are accomplices in it." No other heroine in Shakespeare suffers this kind of exploitation.

—Arthur C. Kirsch, "*Cymbeline* and Coterie Dramaturgy." *English Literary History* 34, no. 3 (September 1967): pp. 285–287, 293–294.

Plot Summary of
The Winter's Tale

The Winter's Tale, probably written along with *Cymbeline* in 1611, had its first recorded performance in May of that year. The main source for this play is Robert Greene's prose-romance entitled *Pandosto,* published around 1588, a literary work familiar to many members of Shakespeare's audience. Greene's story is replete with jealousy, remorse, and the irreversibility of a tragic death. Indeed, the narrative of *Pandosto* begins with the declaration that "among all the passions wherewith human minds are perplexed, there is none that so galleth with restless despite as that infectious sore of jealousy." The Queen in *Pandosto* is accused of "most incestuous adultery," and the story ends in the suicide of the jealous Pandosto, who confesses to having lusted after his own daughter.

Shakespeare reworked this tragic story with many fortuitous reversals of fortune and mythological interventions, all of which transform the potentially tragic events and seemingly hopeless situations into a joyful ending of reunion with loved ones. The peace and harmony restored to the royal family and their subjects is brought about as the result of the characters having learned from past mistakes and misguided passions.

In **Act I,** Camillo, a lord of Sicilia, and Archidamus, a lord of Bohemia, discuss the friendship and the accompanying hospitality to be extended to the visiting King Polixenes of Bohemia, at the court of Leontes in Sicilia. Camillo declares, "Sicilia cannot show himself overkind to Bohemia. They were trained together in their childhoods," to which Archidamus responds, "I think there is not in the world either malice / or matter to alter it." In the next scene, King Polixenes, although Leontes has repeatedly asked that he stay, announces that he will depart Sicilia after an extended visit of nine months' duration, for fear of the consequences of his prolonged absence. He tells Leontes, "I am questioned by my fears of what may chance / Or breed upon our absence, that may blow / No sneaping winds at home." However, Leontes is upset when his entreaties fail, and he becomes fearful that he will be betrayed by the King and his wife.

Leontes raves against the royal couple to his son, Mamillius, giving vent to his suspicions that Polixenes is really an enemy. And, having proclaimed Polixenes the enemy, Leontes next becomes embroiled in a heated discussion about the Queen's virtue, to which Camillo takes great exception, "I would not be a stander-by to hear / My sovereign mistress clouded so without." He then orders Camillo to poison the visiting king, a command which Camillo refuses to carry out.

Act II opens with a pregnant Hermione, Queen to Leontes, speaking with her very precocious son, Mamillius, who is quite astute about women despite his youth. He is given to reading women's faces ("Your brows are blacker; yet black brows, they say, / Become some women best"). Indeed, the young boy, in directing the type of story best suited to entertain the Queen and her ladies, displays the leadership skills he will one day have to assume. "A sad tale's best for winter; I have one / Of sprites and goblins."

Yet, while Mamillius draws the attention of his audience, Leontes continues to rail against the alleged insult he feels by the departure of Polixenes. He then intrudes upon the Queen's entertainment and accuses her of adultery, believing that she has become pregnant with Polixenes's child. Leontes's rage causes him to order the Queen to be imprisoned. To validate his paranoid suspicions, Leontes admits to another of his lords, Antigonus, that he has sent messengers to Delphi to consult with the oracle there. Antigonus, however, dismisses all the suspicion and accusations as ridiculous.

In the meantime, Antigonus's wife, Paulina, visits the imprisoned Hermione and finds that the queen has just given birth to a daughter prematurely. Paulina resolves that she must bring the child to the king in the hope of assuaging his anger and fears. But Leontes is not to be mollified. Instead, his anger is roused at the new affront of Paulina, whom he insults because she has brought the child, which he believes is Polixenes', to mock him.

In **Act III,** Leontes's messengers arrive at Delphos, where the "climate's delicate, the air most sweet," and promising to report on this celestial place, they pray to Apollo to turn all misfortune to right and thereby rescue Hermione. In the meantime, while these entreaties for divine intervention are being made, Leontes's rage continues to escalate, this time causing him to claim that the Queen's alleged infidelity is a crime against the state. In response, she can offer only her own testimony and must rely on her integrity while hoping that there will indeed be divine intervention in her defense.

Shortly thereafter, Cleomenes and Dion return, the messengers of divine deliverance, swearing that they have brought a "sealed-up oracle, by the hand delivered / Of great Apollo's priest," which Leontes promptly opens and reads. "Hermione is chaste, Polixenes blameless, Camillo a true subject, [and] Leontes a jealous tyrant. . . . " Nevertheless, Leontes refuses to accept the message, though admonished by the oracle's advise to mend his ways or "live without an heir."

Shortly thereafter, Leontes hears that his son Mamillius has died because of the injustice done to his mother. Hermione, in response, falls to the ground and is immediately pronounced dead by Paulina. In the face of this tragic news, it now occurs to Leontes that he is indeed the author of his own catastrophes, and in a complete turnaround, he confesses that he has angered the gods. In the meantime, Antigonus has arrived in Bohemia with the new baby whom Hermione, in one of his dreams, has asked him to call Perdita, meaning she who has been lost. Antigonus relates to the baby the contents of his dream. and proclaims that he will never see his own wife again, whom cruel fate has made the "thrower-out" of her Perdita. Pursued by a bear, Antigonus exits.

An old shepherd and his son, a clown [which in its original meaning referred to a country person], now appear to report the death of Antigonus. During the course of this pronouncement, the old shepherd stumbles upon the child and a sack of gold. "Good luck, an't be thy will, what have we here? . . . A very pretty bairn—a boy, or a child, I wonder?"

In **Act IV,** Time plays the part of the chorus and explains what has happened in the interval of sixteen years since Act III. We learn that Leontes has suffered enormous guilt, and that Perdita has grown into a fine young woman under the old shepherd's care, "now grown in grace." In the next scene, at the court of Bohemia, Camillo explains to King Polixenes that he must return home to the court at Sicilia and see the much aggrieved King Leontes. But, before Camillo leaves, there is talk of an affluent shepherd who has raised a lovely daughter and of a rumor that this same daughter has won the affections of young Prince Florizel of Bohemia.

We soon learn that preparations for a sheep-shearing feast are under way and that a clown has been sent to purchase the necessities for the celebration, "three pound of sugar, five pound of currants, rice— what will this sister of mine do with rice? But my father hath made her mistress of the feast." However, along the road the clown is soon beset by the rogue, Autolycus, who is determined to steal the clown's money. While telling a contrived story about being robbed by a notorious rogue, Autolycus succeeds in picking the clown's pocket.

Further on in Act IV, Perdita is wooed by Florizel (disguised as a rustic named Doricles), who eventually confesses that he has been attempting a conceal his love for Perdita from his own father. Polixenes and Doricles are likewise in attendance, albeit in disguise, and Polixenes forbids their union, to which Camillo responds by advising the young lovers to seek refuge with the now repentant Leontes. All of this is done with the help of the charming rogue Autolycus who, disguised as a peddler, exchanges his ragged clothes with the young prince and thus manages to advance his own self-interests while making himself appear benign.

Act V begins in the Sicilian court with Cleomenes begging Leontes to let go of his contrition for his past transgressions. But Leontes remains consumed by guilt for his responsibility in the death of Hermione, for whom he longs in vain. During his lamentations, Paulina reminds him that he has promised to ask her permission before he remarries. "Never, Paulina, so be blessed my spirit." Shortly thereafter, Florizel and Perdita arrive, bearing the news the Polixenes is on his way, giving "all greetings that a king, a friend, / Can send his brother." Nevertheless, it is clear to Florizel that Camillo has betrayed them to Polixenes. And Leontes, sympathetic to the lovers' youth and innocence, decides to plead for the them when Polixenes arrives.

Further on, when Perdita's royal identity is finally revealed by the old shepherd and the clown, the oracle is now complete as the King's daughter is now found. "Such a deal of wonder is broken out within this hour that ballad-makers cannot be able to express it." Even Autolycus thinks it in his best interest to mend his ways, asking the clown to recommend him to the prince. "Pardon me all the faults I have committed to your worship, and to give me your good report to the prince my master."

With all these ruptures repaired and misbehavior amended, it remains for Hermione to make an appearance, which indeed she does, first in the guise of a statue that Paulina has commissioned. But, as it turns out, it is not a "dead likeness" but Hermione herself. She descends from the pedestal on which she stood, brought back to life by Paulina.

And so *The Winter's Tale* ends with husbands and wives reunited with their children. ❀

List of Characters in
The Winter's Tale

Leontes, King of Sicilia. A jealous and suspicious personality who compounds his own problems with each successive accusation of his wife, Hermione, whom he imprisons, and of Polixenes, his guest. In his mad state, Leontes has also sent messengers to consult with the Delphic oracle and when these messengers return to his Court, Leontes refuses to accept the divine message as to the truth of those whom he has falsely and unfairly accused. When he finally begins to see the truth, after being told that his son died due to the cruel treatment of his mother, Leontes confesses that he is the author of his own misfortunes. His response to the overwhelming feelings of guilt cause him to close himself off from the rest of the world. By the time Leontes is finally convinced by others that he has sufficiently repented, he has become a benign and loving King and father.

Hermione. Queen to Leontes, Hermione is falsely accused and cruelly imprisoned by her husband, who believes that she has died as a result of his mistreatment. When it comes to for her to reveal to him that she is indeed alive, she does so in the guise of a statue which Paulina has commissioned.

Mamillius. A very precocious child and devoted son to his mother, Hermione, Mamillius is the young prince of Sicilia. He is very sophisticated in understanding women, and is given to reading their faces. By directing the type of story best suited to entertain the Queen and her ladies, he displays both a sensitivity to their needs and the leadership skills he will one day have to assume.

Perdita. Daughter to Leontes and Hermione. Despite her father's intense feelings of guilt, Perdita has been spared and instead has grown into a fine young woman under the old shepherd's care, "now grown in grace." In Act IV, Perdita is wooed by Florizel (disguised as a man from the country named Doricles) who eventually confesses that he has been attempting a conceal his love for Perdita from his own father. Later on, when Perdita's royal identity is finally revealed, the oracle is now complete as the King's daughter is now found.

Camillo. A Lord of Sicilia. In the beginning of the play, Camillo and Archidamus discuss the friendship and the accompanying hospitality to be extended to the visiting King Polixenes of Bohemia, at the court of Leontes in Sicilia.

Polixenes, King of Bohemia. Anxious that he has stayed so long, Polixenes insists that he must leave for fear of the consequences of his prolonged absence. His refusal to stay any longer invokes Leontes' rage and causes his host to view him as an enemy.

Autolycus. A charming rogue. In Act IV, he is determined to steal the clown's money and does so through a contrived story that he himself has been robbed by a notorious rogue, thus succeeding in picking the clown's pocket. He gladly exhanges his ragged pedlar clothes with Prince Florizel and thus manages to advance his own self-interests while making himself appear benign.

Clown. Son of the Old Shepherd. The original meaning of the word clown was a person from the country. When he is sent to purchase the necessities for a sheep-shearing celebration, he falls prey to Autolycus, who takes advantage of his innocence. ❀

Critical Views of
The Winter's Tale

DARYL W. PALMER ON RUSSIA AND THE
ENGLISH IMAGINATION

[Daryl W. Palmer is the author of *Hospitable Performances: Dramatic Genre and Cultural Practices in Early Modern England* (1992). In this excerpt, Palmer discusses the English imagination and the significance of Russia in terms of both its wintry environment and its stories of royalty, most notably that of Ivan the Terrible.]

Muscovy matters to the English imagination in ways that have scarcely been remarked. To some observers in Jacobean England, mention of the place would have conjured up stories of wintry exploration and icy imperialism, beginning, no doubt, with the image of Sir Hugh Willoughby, frozen along with his company in a Lapland river. Sailing north for Cathay in 1553, Willoughby gave new meaning to the telling of tales in winter. The note detailing his final ice-bound days in the month of September, discovered in one of his two ships, inscribes the event: "Thus remaining in this haven the space of a weeke, seeing the yeare farre spent, & also very evill wether, as frost, snow, and haile, as though it had beene the deepe of winter, we thought best to winter there." Here is a story of winter coming before winter, of winter as fate and alien world, a narrative that breaks off because no one survives to finish it. The cold destruction of this winter's tale meshes in fascinating ways with the narrative of Richard Chancellor, who, having become separated from Willoughby in a tempest, voyaged on to make contact with Ivan the Terrible, emperor of Russia and the embodiment of rough, cold extremes. Chancellor, it was said, had discovered Russia. A flourishing trade developed alongside fragile diplomatic ties. Russian ambassadors visited London in 1557, 1569, 1582, and 1600. A little group of Muscovite students came in 1602 to study at Winchester, Eton, Cambridge, and Oxford. And tales proliferated, so that the mere mention of Muscovites would have brought to mind a picture of this terrible Ivan IV, the burly ruler who proposed marriage to one of Elizabeth's ladies and subsequently chastised the queen for allowing men to rule in her place, for ruling " 'in your maydenlie estate like a maide.' " Muscovy would have suggested the famously unhappy Boris Godunov. It would have triggered images of the wintry port of Archangel, a stormy place of tentlike encampments and of reindeer pulling sleds. Above all, it would have suggested the many narratives of Muscovy Company agents, rehearsed in the pages of Hakluyt and Purchas: stories of the emperor, his customs, jealousies, and violent deeds; accounts of Russian households and ceremonies; chorographies of Russian landscapes; and so on into a wintry prose that stands, I think, as prologue to Shakespeare's *Winter's Tale*.

The play encourages such associations even when it seems focused thematically and geographically elsewhere. When the king of Sicilia accuses his queen "of high treason, in committing adultery with Polixenes, king of Bohemia" (3.2.14–15), Hermione's defense, remarkable both for its pertinence and eloquence, nonetheless exceeds the local terms of Leontes's Sicilia and King James's London. As the court waits breathlessly for the oracle's word, Hermione adds,

> The Emperor of Russia was my father:
> O that he were alive, and here beholding
> His daughter's trial! that he did but see
> The flatness of my misery, yet with eyes
> Of pity, not revenge!
>
> (ll. 119–23)

In the note to line 119 of his Arden edition of the play, J. H. P. Pafford echoes H. B. Charlton, who believes that the Muscovite reference lends "'a sense of majesty and pathos'" to Hermione's plight. Peter Erickson has proposed that "this recourse to the benign father provides a microcosm of the play's resolution." But in its particularity the passage surely demands more aggressive questioning, especially since we know that Shakespeare went out of his way to alter his source so that it was Hermione who would have a Russian father. ⟨ . . . ⟩

The fact that any careful observer could have noticed certain resemblances between the apparently disparate worlds of England and Muscovy seems to have encouraged certain habits of analysis in the pages of Hakluyt and Purchas. To be sure, voyaging led English writers into a host of alien worlds where they developed and refined rhetorical strategies for constructing—even consuming—otherness. Nevertheless, Muscovy posed a special challenge because the region always appeared uncomfortably similar to England; indeed, from their first contact in 1553, English merchants and diplomats have asked their readers to understand Muscovy as an imperfect analogue to England. This analogical thinking underlies both the composition and the reception of Shakespeare's romance. Richard Chancellor inaugurates the convention: "Mosco it selfe is great: I take the whole towne to bee greater then London with the suburbes: but it is very rude, and standeth without all order." Following the same rhetorical plan, he begs his reader to see the emperor of Russia in terms of the English monarch: "then I was sent for againe unto another palace which is called the golden palace, but I saw no cause why it should be so called; for I have seene many fayrer then it in all poynts: and so I came into the hall, which was small and not great as is the Kings Majesties of England." Invoking a favorite notion of the age, we might say that Russia existed as a kind of looking-glass for England and its ruler. The land and its people seemed to encourage projection. So when John Merrick, chief agent for the Muscovy Company, returned to England in the autumn of 1612, he asked James I to envision Russia as his own. Less than a year earlier Shakespeare had toyed with such identifications in *The Winter's Tale*. Now Merrick was proposing that the king make Russia a protectorate, and James fancied the notion. "A King," James asserted, "is trewly *Parens patriae*, the politique father of his people." Perhaps, with his noble prince Henry taken ill, James found comfort in imagining his fatherly duties elsewhere: he would be imposing parental order on the orphaned country. James was still contemplating the project when *The Winter's Tale* was performed at court on the occasion of Princess Elizabeth's wedding in February 1613. For a brief moment it seemed that the English monarch might actually take the place of the emperor of Russia, that the world of fractured courts might merge with the world of happy plays; but the election of Michael Romanov later that same year put an end to this fantasy of Jacobean Muscovites. James never saw his daughter again and hardly spoke to his wife. Any careful observer could have pointed out that none of these reflections had ever been stable.

—Daryl W. Palmer, "Jacobean Muscovites: Winter, Tyranny, and Knowledge in *The Winter's Tale*." *Shakespeare Quarterly* 46, no. 3 (Fall 1995): pp. 323–324, 326–327.

[Nevill Coghill is a very well-known scholar. His books include *The Poet Chaucer* (1950) and *Shakespeare's Professional Skills* (1964). In the excerpt below, Coghill discusses Shakespeare's skill and inventiveness as a storyteller in the way he represents Leontes' "supposed suddenness."]

Shakespeare's stage-craft in this play is as novel, subtle and revolutionary as it had been a few years before in *Antony and Cleopatra,* but in an entirely different way: just as he had then found the technical path to an actual and life-sized world—to the drums and tramplings of the Roman Empire—so, in *The Winter's Tale* he hit upon a means of entry into the fabulous world of a life standing (as Hermione says) in the level of dreams.

Stage-craft is a word for the mechanics in the art of telling a story, through actors, on some sort of stage, *with a certain effect.* It must inventively use the facilities available to it. No one was more inventive than Shakespeare: deftness and dexterity of this kind mark all his work, and his surprises (so often, afterwards, felt to be 'inevitable') recall those in Beethoven, of whose last quartets the composer Balfour Gardiner said once to me, with a sigh of envy, "Ah, the desolating old monkey! Never without a fresh rabbit to pull out of his hat!" ⟨ . . . ⟩

I. The Supposed Suddenness of the Jealousy of Leontes

> In *Pandosto* (we shall use Shakespeare's names) Leontes' jealousy is made slow and by increase plausible. Shakespeare weakens the plausibility of it as well by ennobling Hermione—after his way with good women—as by huddling up the jealousy in its motion so densely that it strikes us as merely frantic and—which is worse in drama—a piece of impossible improbability. This has always and rightly offended the critics. . . . (Sir Arthur Quiller-Couch).
>
> Then suddenly with no more hint of preparation—and no hint at all on the psychological plane—Leontes' jealousy comes full upon him (S. L. Bethell).

In an appendix devoted to this subject Bethell adds the conjecture that if Shakespeare had intended Leontes to be jealous from the start he would have brought him on alone "to deliver an appropriate soliloquy". This would indeed have been "a naïve and outmoded technique", one at least as old-fashioned as that which, long before, had so brilliantly opened *Richard III.* But in *The Winter's Tale* Shakespeare went about his business with new subtlety of dramatic invention. To understand it we must begin at the opening scene, a dialogue between Archidamus and Camillo, asking ourselves certain questions in dramaturgy.

What is the reason for this dialogue? What information does it convey? What is it supposed to do to an audience? At first sight it seems to resemble the opening scenes of *King Lear* and *Antony and Cleopatra:* just as Kent and Gloucester prepare us for the division of Lear's kingdom and introduce the Bastard, just as Philo and Demetrius announce Antony's dotage and prepare us to see him enter as a strumpet's fool, so Archidamus and Camillo prepare us to witness a kingly amity between Sicilia and Bohemia, his guest, and to introduce us to Mamillius. There is no other point in the little scene:

> *Cam.* Sicilia cannot show himself over-kind to Bohemia. They were trained together in childhoods; and there rooted betwixt them such an affection, which cannot choose but branch now . . . they have seemed to be rooted together, though absent, shook hands, as over a vast, and embraced, as it were, from the ends of opposed winds. The heavens continue their loves!
>
> *Arch.* I think there is not in the world either malice or matter to alter it. You have an unspeakable comfort of your young prince Mamillius . . . (I, i, 23–38)

Now whereas Kent and Gloucester, Philo and Demetrius, prepare the audience for what it is about to see (technique of gratifying expectation raised), Camillo and Archidamus prepare it for what it is about *not* to see (technique of the prepared surprise): directed to expect a pair of happy and affectionate friends, the audience is startled by seeing exactly the opposite: the two monarchs enter separately, and one, perceived to be the other's host, wears a look of barely controlled hostility that may at any moment blacken into a thundercloud. The proof of this is in the dialogue, which contains all the stage-directions necessary; Polixenes leads in with his elaborate lines:

> Nine changes of the watery star hath been
> The shepherd's note since we have left our throne
> Without a burthen: time as long again
> Would be fill'd up, my brother, with our thanks;
> And yet we should, for perpetuity.
> Go hence in debt: and therefore, like a cipher,
> Yet standing in rich place, I multiply
> With one 'We thank you' many thousands moe
> That go before it.
>
> (I, ii, 1–9)

Polixenes is an artist in the language of court compliment, at once flowery and formal, like Jacobean embroidery. All the flourish of his opening lines conveys no more information than this: "*I am visiting the King and have been here nine months.*" His closing lines, however, make it certain that he is standing beside Hermione (she is perhaps upon his arm?) and addressing her. With self-deprecating paronomasia, and a bow no doubt, he pays her compliment:

> And therefore, *like a cipher,*
> *Yet standing in rich place.* . . .

To a visiting King there can be no richer place than next to the Queen. This Queen, however, has something specially remarkable about her: she is *visibly pregnant,* and near her hour, for a day later we hear the First Lady tell Mamillius:

> The queen your mother rounds apace.
> (II, i, 16)

This fact about her has been grasped by the audience at her first entry, because they can see it is so; they hear the visiting King say he has been there nine months; who can fail to wonder whether the man so amicably addressing this expectant mother may not be the father of her child? For what other possible reason can Shakespeare have contrived the conversation so as to make him specify nine changes of the inconstant moon? These things are not done by accident; Shakespeare has established a complex situation with the same inerrant economy, swiftness, and originality that he used to open *Hamlet* or *Macbeth.*

> —Nevill Coghill. "Six Points of Stage-Craft in *The Winter's Tale,*" *Shakespeare Survey* 11 (1958): pp. 31–33.

☙

Charles R. Forker on the Paradoxes of Art and Nature

[Charles R. Forker is the author of *Fancy's Images: Contexts, Settings, and Perspectives in Shakespeare and His Contemporaries* (1990) and *Skull Beneath the Skin: The Achievement of*

John Webster (1986). In the excerpt below, Forker discusses how an understanding of intense psychological states of mind mediates the opposition between the natural and the supernatural in *The Winter's Tale.*]

Like all the romances of Shakespeare, *The Winter's Tale* is a subtle compound of the fantastic and the verisimilar, the improbable and the credible, the ideal and the real, the mythic and the naturalistic. In my experience, undergraduate and, on occasion, even graduate students often need some help in accepting a theatrically mixed mode that invokes the narrative traditions of the folktale (with its implications of strangeness, artificiality, and distancing from ordinary experience) but that nevertheless insists on a high degree of dramatic engagement; that, treating potentially tragic characters and situations, represents intense psychological states and embodies serious moral, aesthetic, and philosophical ideas.

Shakespeare stresses one side of this opposition not only in his title but in details of the dialogue—in Mamillius's reference, for example, to stories of "sprites and goblins" (2.1.26) and in the Second Gentleman's allusion to tales the "verity" of which would be "in strong suspicion" (5.2.29–30); these references have the effect of italicizing the romance conventions and miraculous vicissitudes in which the plot abounds. The apparently "broken-backed" structure of the play, with its three acts of pain and disaster followed by two in which new characters are introduced and in which the former misery is transmuted into present joy—the contrasting sections being joined somewhat perfunctorily by the chorus Time, who in a single speech leaps blithely over a gap of sixteen years—also reinforces the sense of a play that is consciously anachronistic, "antique" or "storied" in dramaturgy and deliberately antinaturalistic in appeal. Yet the volcanic eruption of Leontes's jealousy, the powerful episode in which Hermione publicly defends her innocence, and the action in which Paulina reveals the statue and presides over its quasi-mystical vivification have the very opposite effect; for these scenes engage audience emotions strongly and directly, leaving little leisure for fanciful detachment, and they depend on characters whose inner being is not only imagined in depth but rivetingly actualized in stage performance. Merely noticing this mixture of modes can help focus students' attention on some of the play's more absorbing interpretive problems—problems that, when more fully investigated and discussed, can sometimes convince the less sophisticated that what they may have perceived initially as a loose collection of naïve, confused, or absurd elements on closer inspection composes a richly complex web of actions, characters, and symbols possesssing coherence and even profundity.

An obvious way of overcoming resistance to the apparently diffuse or desultory aspects of the plot is to have students consider the matrix of thematic and symbolic contrasts that the play clearly projects—age and youth, winter and summer, court and country, aristocracy and peasantry, death and resurrection, sin and redemption, decay and growth, innocence and guilt, suspicion and trust, tyranny and freedom, love and friendship, sadness and joy, time and eternity, life and art—and then to suggest how these mesh and overlap, often through simultaneous opposition and parallel. In its two halves, for instance, the drama clearly shifts its emphasis from the older generation to the younger, yet children are already present in the early segment just as adults figure in the concluding one; and although progeny are certainly meant to be associated with continuity and life (as in the case of Perdita and Florizel), the death of Mamillius and the "resurrection" of Hermione show us that biological age is too simple and inadequate a means of symbolizing the tension between fruitfulness and mortality. Moreover, Shakespeare appears to invite very different responses to death: the wasting away of Leontes's son in the early action evokes tragic emotions and seems to connote irreparable loss, not only of the boy but of all that is morally and psychologically healthful, whereas the predatory devouring of Antigonus later on, while equally irreparable, is filtered semicomically through the narrative of the clown, who describes the event as a grotesque meal at which "the bear half din'd on the gentleman" (3.3.102–03). Much of the comedy of the play, as the example just cited, depends on traditional contrasts between the humbly and the nobly born, but nobility and peasantry obviously intersect in the country royalty of Perdita, who is both a "queen of curds and cream" (4.4.161) and the future consort of a monarch.

The thematic polarities of the play, like the early and late phases of its action, tend to contain each other in embryo or in retrospect, one term already implying or helping to define its counterpart, in the same way that Milton's "L'Allegro" and "Il Penserso" must be properly understood as conceptually related poems rather than as discrete works. Shakespeare's pervasive dualities suggest the complimentarity and indivisibility of experience rather than its fission into mutually exclusive units, and some discussion of these cross-relations can bring the structural and intellectual subtleties of the play into clearer focus.

An opening pedagogical gambit I find useful is to pursue the question of how audiences are intended to receive the abruptness of Leontes's jealousy in the first act and its almost equally abrupt abandonment in the third. It is usual of course to say with F. R. Leavis (and many others) that we should neither look for nor expect in a fairy tale the "psychological interest" found in *Othello,* that in generic romance, such fits of irrationality are "notoriously unmotivated" (Bethell 48) and can descend and evaporate as arbitrarily as supernatural spells or diabolic possession. Yet it is possible (as with Wilbur Sanders) to analyze the triangular relationship of Leontes, Polixenes, and Hermione as hinting at complex patterns of suppressed tension, insecurity, and discomfort such as one might find in a novel by Henry James. Polixenes, for instance, finds it awkward to extend his stay in the court of a boyhood friend whom he has only recently come to know as an adult, whose grown-up reality may cause him to exaggerate nostalgically—even sentimentally—the innocence of their youthful attachment, and whose attractive wife and son remind him of his own pressing obligations of family and state at home. For his part, Leontes reveals a perverse tendency to associate every human failing with sexuality, so that almost any evil, however hypothetical, takes on a repellent lubricity in his prurient imagination. Whether or not one accepts all the psychological sutbtleties Sanders describes, he at least makes a good case for regarding the scenes of jealousy as symptomatic of the play's mixed mode: certainly "we can make out the mythic triumph of wickedness, the paradigm of fairy tale. But," Sanders continues, "this co-exists with, and is empowered by, a psychological naturalism of quite amazing depth and resourcefulness." We may therefore add to the thematic and structural contrasts that encourage bifocal responses to *The Winter's Tale* a certain doubleness in the characterization—a means of presenting the central figures so as to give the illusion of fully rounded personality without sacrificing any of their larger symbolic or archetypal functions.

—Charles R. Forker, "Negotiating the Paradoxes of Art and Nature in *The Winter's Tale.*" In *Approaches to Teaching Shakespeare's The Tempest and Other Late Romances,* ed. Maurice Hunt (New York: The Modern Language Association of America, 1992): pp. 94–96.

[Stephen Orgel is the author of *Impersonations: The Performance of Gender in Shakespeare's England* (1996) and *The Jon-
sonian Masque* (1965). In the excerpt below from his edition
of *The Winter's Tale,* Orgel discusses the problems of the play
for the modern audience.]

The play's problems for a modern audience are not, of course, merely
generic. They are in every sense dramatic, the more so if one is aware of
Shakespeare's earlier treatments of similar issues. Why does he set up the
powerful tragic momentum of the opening three acts, only to disarm it
with fantasy and magic? Why is Mamillius not restored, along with
Hermione and Perdita; and moreover, why is the death of Mamillius—
Leontes' only son and the heir to the throne—so much less of an issue
dramatically than the death of his wife and the loss of his daughter? Perhaps most puzzling of all, why does Shakespeare preserve Leontes and
ultimately exonerate him—why is he not treated in the fashion of all
those other foolish, headstrong, misguided, tyrannical Shakespearian
kings, who go to their deaths even in those cases where it is acknowl-
edged that they are more sinned against than sinning? In fact, if we read
The Winter's Tale in the context of Shakespeare's earlier dramas of royalty, we will be struck by how little distinction is normally accorded to
the office of king, how close the dread sovereign is to the foolish, fond
old man. There are in *Hamlet* no claims about the particular sanctity of
kingship, nor is the murder of an anointed king represented as more
heinous than the murder of anybody else. *Macbeth* does make claims
about the murder of Duncan, but not about the killing of Macbeth, who
is no less a duly anointed king; and more significantly, the play has no in-
vestment in making the king a good king—in educating Duncan in the
proper management of his thanes and his realm, in rehabilitating Macbeth through penance, prayer, and the advice of a good woman, in ensuring that Malcolm will not repeat Duncan's mistakes by taking as his
right-hand man a dubiously ethical soldier like Macduff. Why then, the
intense focus on the preservation and rehabilitation of Leontes? Why not
let him atone by dying, and resolve the tragic issues through the acces-
sion of a new and innocent generation, on the models provided by the
endings of *2 Henry IV, Macbeth* and *King Lear?* Shakespeare's source, indeed, gave him a strikingly dramatic model: at the conclusion of Greene's

Pandosto, the repentant king falls in love with his still unidentified daughter; and when he learns who she is, kills himself, to be succeeded on the throne by his unsullied daughter and son-in-law. This is an ending that would be perfectly consistent with the tragedy of royalty as Shakespeare practised it, and both the preservation of Leontes and the mode by which it is effected are unique in his drama.

The play is problematic, too, in a more specific and local sense. It is syntactically and lexically often baffling, though this is an aspect of the text that has been generally ignored by editors and critics since about the middle of the last century. But if we consider the editorial debates over such passages as Polixenes' explanation of his need to return home (1.2.12–15), Hermione's protestations at her trial (3.2.45–50 and 103–4), most of all, Leontes' jealous ravings (1.2.136–44, and elsewhere), it is clear that even where a consensus has been reached, it is based on no real linguistic evidence. Here are two examples.

Hermione, in the course of her objections to her treatment, says to Leontes,

> I appeal
> To your own conscience, sir, before Polixenes
> Came to your court how I was in your grace,
> How merited to be so; since he came,
> With what encounter so uncurrent I
> Have strained t'appear thus . . .
>
> (3.2.44–9)

For the past hundred years or so, the last two lines have been taken to mean 'with what behavior so unacceptable I have transgressed that I should appear thus (i.e. on trial)'. This interpretation represents the consensus of three mid-Victorian editors, Haliwell, Staunton and White, and it has become, for us, simply the meaning of the passage. But to gloss the passage in this way is, at the very least, to conceal more than a century of debate and bafflement. The lines were, in fact, considered incomprehensible by most eighteenth-century editors including Johnson, who wrote of them, 'These lines I do not understand; with the licence of all editors, what I cannot understand I suppose unintelligible and therefore propose that they may be altered . . . ' Johnson's testimony in this matter is especially apropos, given his characteristic genius for finding a plain prose sense in the most elaborately conceited Shakespearian verse. In default of an interpretation, he produced a felicitous, if unconvincingly rationalized, emendation: 'With what encounter so uncurrent *have I* | *Been stained* to appear thus?' Even this, though it certainly makes a kind of sense, depends on its emendation to render the crucially ambiguous words *encounter* and *uncurrent* comprehensible. A detailed consideration of the history of similar attempts at elucidation would show no more than the relevant *OED* entries, for *encounter, uncurrent,* and *strain:* that the modern interpretation represents an essentially arbitrary selection of meanings from a list of diverse and often contradictory possibilities, and does not so much resolve the linguistic problem as enable us to ignore it. The confident tone of the gloss conveying this interpretation will give no hint of two centuries of uncertainty, debate and disagreement.

—Stephen Orgel, ed. Introduction to *The Winter's Tale,* by William Shakespeare. (Oxford: Clarendon Press, 1996): pp. 6–8.

☙

CHARLES FREY ON THE TRAGIC STRUCTURE OF *THE WINTER'S TALE*

[Charles Frey is the author of *The Literary Heritage of Childhood: An Appraisal of Children's Classics in the Western Tradition* (1987) and *Experiencing Shakespeare: Essays on Text, Classroom and Performance* (1988). In the excerpt below, Frey focuses on the darker and more serious aspects of Shakespeare's romance plays.]

To judge by the classifications of plays in the First Folio, Shakespeare's colleagues, if not Shakespeare himself, thought *The Winter's Tale* and *The Tempest* comedies and *Cymbeline* a tragedy. Of *Pericles,* it seems, they scarcely thought at all, for that play was omitted from their collection. Only after two hundred and fifty years of study were the four plays identified as written consecutively and late in Shakespeare's career. When, about a century ago, scholars began to term the plays "romances" and then even to group them, in collected editions, under that separate heading, they opened a brilliant chapter in Shakespearean interpretation. Not only did the generic label "romance" suggest that there were significant correlations among the plays—correlations which might set them off from all the rest in the fashion that "problem" plays or "Roman" plays are sometimes set off—but also the focus upon romance suggested the special relevance of a literary tradition invested with awesome age, universality, and power.

Romance, the dominant mode of fiction-making numbering among its heroes Odysseus, Alcestis, Apollonius of Tyre, the knights of Charlemagne and Arthur, protagonists of Spenser, Sidney, Greene, Cervantes, and thousands more, usually tells, of course, the elemental story of journey and, sometimes, of return. Return, forgiveness, and reconciliation are much stressed in Shakespeare's romance, and those who, like Edward Dowden, first applied the term did so to suggest the plays' aura of post-tragic acceptance and benign spirituality:

> Characteristics of versification and style, and the enlarged place given to scenic spectacle, indicate that these plays were produced much about the same time. But the ties of deepest kinship between them are spiritual. There is a certain romantic element in each. They receive contributions from every portion of Shakespeare's genius, but all are mellowed, refined, made exquisite; they avoid the extremes of broad humour and of tragic intensity; they were written with less of passionate concentration than the plays which immediately precede them, but with more of a spirit of deep or exquisite recreation.

Today, while we are grateful for the insights of an earlier age into Shakespeare's recreative spirit of romance, we may doubt that he eschewed "tragic intensity" or that he wrote these plays with less than "passionate concentration." We are, indeed, rediscovering for ourselves both the seriousness and craft of romance, and we are finding in the vaults of Shakespeare's late plays both dark chambers to be explored and curious treasures that may defy the light. ⟨ . . . ⟩

Whether or not we understand its origins, separation of wives and daughters from husbands and home remains a chief feature of Shakespearean romance, and some sort of familial over-closeness, real or imagined, often initiates the action. We need to explore more fully how the romances portray man's mistrust and mistreatment of woman and with what dramatic impact. In *The Winter's Tale,* the jealousy of Leontes and its consequences are made manifest through a passionate concentration of forms that reach, surely, that tragic intensity Dowden denied to the romances.

During the first three acts of *The Winter's Tale,* Leontes appears four times and each time does the same thing: he denounces Hermione or her surrogate, Paulina, and is rebuked by representatives of his court. To be more precise, in a theme with little variation, Leontes four times expresses his misogyny, separates mother from child, and confronts indignant by-standers. Even if the play were dumb show, this reenacted emblem of blighted affection would work deep into the consciousness of spectators.

During his first appearance onstage (I.ii), Leontes watches Hermione as she holds Polixenes' hand; they withdraw from him, and soon he dismisses Mamillius. His violent argument with Camillo follows. In the third scene, he comes upon Hermione and Mamillius, pulls the boy from her, forces them to separate exits, and faces the rebukes of Antigonus and the lords. In the seventh scene, the trial scene, Leontes attacks Hermione, loses Mamillius and her, and suffers the stinging rebuke of Paulina.

The purpose of this reduplicating structure is not primarily to advance the plot, nor is it to explore the motivations of the king. It serves instead to amplify the dimensions of his nightmare and to demonstrate in wider ambit the consequences of his condition. An audience will persist in finding Leontes mad, but will find it harder and harder to ignore the implications of that madness. His idiom spawns violence, and the audience sees an increasingly violent series of expulsions:

> Bear the boy hence.
> (II.i.59)
> Away with her, to prison!
> (II.i.103)
> Go, do our bidding; hence!
> (II.i.125)
> Leave me solely; go.
> (II.iii.17)
> Away with that audacious lady!
> (II.iii.42)
> Hence with her, out o' door!
> (II.iii.68)
> Will you not push her out?
> (II.iii.74)

As the audience hears Leontes conceive his jealousy, accuse Hermione, debate Paulina, and conduct the trial, it also sees him rejecting advice, dismissing women, losing company, being left alone, so that, while he orally projects an image of alienated man, he iconographically enacts the part as well.

—Charles Frey, "Tragic Structure in *The Winter's Tale:* The Affective Dimension." In *Shakespeare's Romances Reconsidered,* ed. Carol McGinnis Kay and Henry E. Jacobs (Lincoln: University of Nebraska Press, 1978): pp. 113–116.

Plot Summary of
The Tempest

The most important sources for *The Tempest* are *The Bermuda Pamphlets,* a variety of travelogues and sermons dealing with the New World, such as the *Discovery of the Barmudas* (1610) and the *True Declaration of the state of the Colonie of Virginia,* and, to a lesser extent, Montaigne's essay "Of Cannibals." Collectively, these works influenced the Renaissance interest in exploration of the New World. This interest was accompanied by a fascination with native populations and how they responded to the encroachment by "civilized" cultures.

The Bermuda Pamphlets describe the shipwreck of the *Sea-Adventure,* a ship which carried five hundred colonists to Virignia Colony. While caught in a storm, the crew were forced to run their ship ashore, but all on board managed to land safely. The *True Declaration of the state of the Colonie of Virginia,* issued for propaganda purposes, emphasizes the abundance to be found in the New World and illustrates the need to trust in God, a theme Shakespeare incorporates in *The Tempest* when the happy shipwreck delivers the passengers to a place of safe haven. Finally, Montaigne's essay raises the issue of the "natural" man in comparison to members of an artificial or "civilized" society. Montaigne has great sympathy for the natural man as demonstrated in this essay. "Now . . . I finde (as farre as I have beene informed) there is nothing in that nation, that is either barbarous or savage, unlese men call that barbarisme which is not common to them. . . . There is ever perfect religion, perfect policie, perfect and compleat use of all things."

Act I opens upon a chaotic scene, "all lost to prayers, caught up in a tempestuous storm at sea," the mariners battling the elements and Gonzalo, an honest old counselor, wishing for death on dry land. To make matters even more tumultuous, the mariners must contend with obstreperous members of the royal court, including Antonio, the usurping Duke of Milan, and Sebastian, a brother to the King of Naples, who are returning to Italy from Tunis following a royal wedding. Emotions on board are as intense as the raging storm as Antonio declares he and his entourage "are merely cheated of our lives by drunkards."

However, the violence of weather and emotion quickly shift with the venue of the next scene, that of the "uninhabited island" where Prospero, the magician-father and rightful Duke of Milan, is standing before his "cell" with his daughter Miranda. Wondering whether Prospero is responsible for this seeming calamity, Miranda asks him to calm "the wild waters," to which he assures her that all is well and nothing is to be feared from this "direful spectacle," which he has caused through his magic. Furthermore, he tells his daughter about her true and noble birth and the circumstances by which both father and daughter have been cheated of their royal status and possessions. Prospero's brother, Antonio, appropriated power for himself because Prospero was preoccupied with books; thus the magician allowed himself to be seduced by his own love of "secret studies" and the improvement of his mind. He relates to Miranda how they were set adrift in a leaky boat and helped by fortune and the graces of the goodly Gonzalo, who filled the boat with all manner of food and provisions, to reach the safety of the deserted island on which they now live. Fortune has now delivered Prospero's enemies directly into the magician's hands, to which Prospero responds by putting Miranda to sleep and summoning a spirit that he controls, Ariel.

Though Ariel asks Prospero to make good on his promise to free him, reminding Prospero that he has done him "worthy service," Prospero intends to keep Ariel a little longer in his service by reminding him of a debt he owes his master, who saved him from the evil witch Sycorax. This witch was banished "[f]or mischiefs manifold, and sorceries terrible" and was responsible for confining Ariel in a "cloven pine" with the hope of leaving the island to her son Caliban. Ariel's work is not done; he must disguise himself "like a nymph 'o th' sea" and continue to do Prospero's bidding.

When Miranda awakens, she and her father go off to see Caliban, now a slave, though Miranda protests that she has no desire to see him. They meet with a torrent of verbal abuse, and Caliban declares that the island rightfully belongs to his mother, Sycorax, and that he is therefore in charge. However, he is soon reminded by Prospero that he has been enslaved for the crime of threatening Miranda's virginity.

Following this angry scene, Act I ends with Miranda falling in love with Ferdinand, prince of Naples. Her love is reciprocated by Ferdinand, who proclaims that she is "[m]ost sure the goddess / On whom these airs attend." Prospero, however, plans to intervene, lest the young prince too easily win his daughter. "They are both in either's pow'rs: but this / swift business / I must uneasy make, lest to light winning / Make the prize light."

At the beginning of **Act II,** Gonzalo and the other members of the royal party express awe and amazement at their survival ("[B]ut for the miracle, / I mean our preservation, few in millions / Can speak like us"). This joy leads Gonzalo to thoughts about the ideal government of equality for all its citizens ("I' th' commonwealth I would by contraries / Execute all things . . . riches, poverty, / And use of service, none . . . all men ideal, all; / And women too"). While Gonzalo describes the ideal commonwealth, Sebastian and Antonio make fun of the wise old counselor.

After this, Ariel lulls Gonzalo and Alonso to sleep, while Sebastian and Antonio plan to murder King Alonso and the wise old counselor. Fortunately, Gonzalo awakens in time to summon divine intervention ("now, good angels / Preserve the King!") and thereby thwart the plot before it can be acted upon.

Before Act II is concluded, the drunken clowns, Stephan and Trinculo, separated from their own master, encounter the foul-mouthed Caliban and attempt to persuade him to become their servant. Caliban is all too easily duped and ready to do their bidding. The three leave the stage singing "freedom, high-day! High-day, freedom!"

In **Act III,** Ferdinand, obeying Prospero's demands for service, is made to carry and stack wooden logs, despite Miranda's protests that he should cease his heavy toil. During this scene, the lovers reaffirm their devotion and the inexperienced Miranda proposes marriage to Ferdinand. All of this takes place under Propsero's manipulative and approving eye. "So glad of this as they I cannot be . . . but my rejoicing / At nothing can be more."

Meanwhile, in sharp contrast to Ferdinand and Miranda's exchanging vows of loving service to one another, in the next scene Caliban plots with his two drunken companions. The three conspire to kill Prospero while he sleeps, as Caliban advises them on what to do. "There thou mayst brain him, / Having first seiz'd his books; . . . for without them / He's but a sot." However, Ariel is invisible and is thus able to eavesdrop undetected. Ariel plays a tune on a tablor (a stringed instrument) and pipe, and throws the three rascals into a state of confusion, with Caliban trying to calm their nerves. "Be not afeard; the isle is full of noises, / . . . Sometimes a thousand twangling instruments / Will hum about mine ears."

To add to the diverse events on this island, there is yet a third scene in which the royal party stops to rest, under the direction and control of the master magician. Prospero causes a strange and solemn music to entice the unsuspecting group into becoming unwitting participants at a banquet. He becomes the stage manager of his own script, as he boasts of his power to Ariel. But in another marvelous turn of events, the banquet ends with the participants hearing dreadful sounds of wind and thunder, all of which haunt them with their "great guilt, / Like poison given to work a great time after."

In **Act IV,** the mythological gods play a significant role. The scene begins with Prospero promising Miranda's hand in marriage, with the proviso that Ferdinand respect her virtue. Prospero next orders Ariel to gather the lesser spirits, "O'er whom I give thee power" to convince the young lovers of Prospero's magic. That display takes the form a wedding masque. A masque was a Renaissance dramatic genre which developed in Italy; masked and ornately costumed figures, representing mythological or symbolic beings, entertained a noble house or royal court with singing and dancing. Research indicates that the masque's themes revolved around the sources and conditions of power. Despite its aristocratic associations, however, the masque also developed from various types of street entertainment in Europe. Therefore, by implication, the masque included common people as well. Shakespeare's inclusion of the masque as a play within a play alludes to classical themes and Greek mythological gods—Juno (the wife of Jupiter and patroness of marriage and the well-being of women), Iris (goddess of the rainbow and messenger of the gods), and Ceres (goddess of growth and agriculture).

The inclusion of the masque within *The Tempest* is also a demonstration of Prospero's directorial skills, as he manipulates of the characters of the masque as well as the courtship of the two young lovers. Prospero's manipulation is exemplified in such instances as his directions to Juno and Ceres, where he advises them to "whisper seriously;/ There's something else to do: hush, and be mute, / Or else our spell is marr'd." While musicians and dancers attend Iris, Juno, and Ceres appear, promising the couple fertility in the coming years. However, the masque is abruptly ended when Prospero is reminded of Caliban's scheme.

Prospero must now direct his attention to the impending calamity wrought by this devil and his newly-acquired friends, Trinculo and Stephano. Once again, Ariel is summoned, this time dressed in glittering apparel, to tempt the villains. He creates a wonderful wardrobe that distracts Trinculo and Stephano, although Caliban suspects trickery. Added to Ariel's ruse is the noise of hunters and the entry of various spirits in the shape of dogs and hounds.

Act V opens with Prospero praising his own abilities to direct the plot and its characters according to his own wishes. "Now does my project gather to a head: / My charms crack not; my spirits obey; and time / Goes upright." At the same time, Ariel reminds Prospero of the condition of his captives, the usurping Duke and his retinue, and predicts that the sight of them, especially of the "the good old lord" Gonzalo, will soften Prospero's feelings. Ariel is correct, and Prospero offers mercy in exchange for the return of his political status and the privilege of seeing him work his magical charms.

That "wonder" is immediately presented in the next scene when Miranda and Ferdinand play chess, while Alonso is reunited with his son, whom he thought perished at sea. The game of chess is significant, for it offered a space to medieval lovers where they would be permitted equality of the sexes and freedom of expression. (As is noted in the Arden edition of *The Tempest,* edited by Frank Kermode, "chess games between lovers are frequently represented on wedding-chest and mirror-cases.")

Finally, the last to be freed are Caliban and his companions, an act of such generosity given the evil they had previously intended, that it causes the "mis-shapen knave" to declare of Prospero, "How fine my master is!" Thus the play ends with Prospero, having set Ariel free, asking for the same favor. These lines occur at the end of the Epilogue and, as Frank Kermode notes, have been at "the heart of the controversy of the play as a personal allegory. It is on the whole more plausible to treat them as an apology to James I 'for dabbling in magic.'" Alternatively, the Epilogue can be understood as an appeal for approval, the same self-congratulation which Prospero has indulged in several times throughout the play, but an approval which is granted as a recognition of the good he has done. ❀

List of Characters in
The Tempest

Prospero, the Duke of Milan is the magician-father of Miranda who orchestrates the shipwreck in Act I. Prospero and Miranda lost both their royal position and their possessions because of his brother Antonio and his supporters, and in part because Prospero was preoccupied with his studies. This character is resemblance to the alchemist, a figure in Renaissance literature who was a symbol of the inherent dangers of dabbling in arcane matters. In many ways, Propsero is the theatrical manager of *The Tempest* and in his epilogue at the conclusion of Act V Prospero makes an appeal to the audience to forgive him for the "rough magic" he has wrought.

Miranda is daughter to Prospero. When Prospero discloses Miranda's true nobility and the circumstances that lead to their habitation of the island, she falls into a deep sleep induced "strangeness" of Prospero's story. A little further on, Miranda once again falls under her father's spell when she first sets eyes on Ferdinand, and Prospero maintains control of the relationship. In Act IV, Prospero promises Miranda's hand in marriage and orders a great theatrical display in the service of promoting their romance.

In Act I, Alonso's brother **Sebastian** and Antonio (the usurping Duke of Milan), both members of the "illegitimate" court of Milan, plan to murder King Alonso and the wise and benevolent old counsellor, Gonzalo, towards whom Sebastian is very disrespectful. Sebastian is an evil character who has befriended the conniving and usurping Antonio and one who both encourages and thrives on political intrigue.

Antonio is Prospero's brother and the usurping Duke of Milan. Antonio and Sebastian are forever making derisive remarks about Gonzalo. Antonio mocks Gonzalo in his wish for a true commonwealth in which all citizens are equal. And, in contrast to Gonzalo, Antonio protests his complete satisfaction in appropriating Prospero's dukedom.

Alonso, King of Naples is on board ship with his royal entourage during a tumultuous storm at sea. Although he is not one of the major characters in the play, we soon learn from Prospero that Alonso is one of his enemies, in that he supports Antonio's political agenda to become the Duke of Milan and, indeed, he is responsible for opening the city gates to Alonzo and for allowing the ministers to abduct Propsero and Miranda. During the shipwreck, Alonso is separated from his son Ferdinand and believes his son to be dead. In Act II, this supposed loss becomes even more poignant when he is reminded of his daughter, Dido, who has become the Queen of Tunis. At the end of Act III, due to Ariel's magic, Alonso believes that the very sea calls out the name "Prosper" to remind him of his grief and does indeed cause the King to go mad. In the beginning of Act V, Alonso is at first incredulous that he is actually standing before Prospero but after granting Prospero his dukedom, Prospero responds with an equally generous gesture by granting him a reunion with his son Ferdinand. And, thus, Alsono's worst fears are allayed.

Ferdinand is son to the King of Naples. In Act I, Ferdinand jumps overboard from the doomed ship, believing it to be possessed by the devil. Under Prospero's direction, Ferdinand falls helplessly in love with Miranda. However, Prospero decides that he must first prove himself worthy of Miranda and, thus, Ferdinand is subjected to heavy labor. In Act V, Ferdinand declares that Propsero has bestowed two blessings upon him—he has saved him from the shipwreck and has become his second father.

In Act I, Prospero tells Miranda how the kind-hearted **Gonzalo** had filled their boat with food and provisions, thus ensuring their safe arrival at the deserted island on which they now live. In expressing his gratitude for the safe landing of the royal party, Gonzalo's thankfulness leads to thoughts about the ideal government in which all citizens would be equal. In Act V, the thought of this trusted old counselor causes Prospero to soften his feelings against all those who conspired against him.

Caliban is a savage and deformed slave, son of the evil witch Sycorax (who had been banished for her terrible sorceries). Though Caliban declares that the island rightfully belongs to his mother, Sycorax, and that he is therefore in charge, he is soon reminded by Prospero that he has been enslaved for the crime of threatening Miranda's virginity. Before Act II is concluded, the drunken clowns, Stephan and Trinculo, prey on the easily duped Caliban, and attempt to persuade him into becoming their servant. Indeed, their powers of persuasion go so far that they convince Caliban to conspire with them to kill Prospero while he sleeps. Eventually, all three rogues are freed in an display of Prospero's great generosity.

Ariel is an airy spirit that Prospero claims is indebted to him because Prospero rescued Ariel from the evil witch Sycorax, who had confined the spirit in a tree. In exchange for this help, Prospero keeps Ariel in his service. As a spirit of the air, Ariel is invisible and thus able to eavesdrop undetected and play tricks on people. At the end of the play, Ariel is finally set free. ❁

Critical Views on
The Tempest

> [In this article, L.T. Fitz discusses the conflicting imagery be-
> tween the "hostile" environment of Prospero's island and that
> of the images of a "cultivated Nature" in the masque.]

In this day of travel bureaus and the *National Geographic,* it is easy to
form preconceived notions of what Prospero's island looks like. We
summon up visions of Samoa or Tahiti or other tropical paradises and
impose the visions back on *The Tempest.* We are encouraged in this
task of the imagination by our knowledge of the Bermuda pamphlets
and our knowledge or daydreams of present-day Bermuda. ⟨ . . . ⟩ The
problem is that there are no oleander hedges in *The Tempest;* there are
not even any palm trees (that prime requisite for a modern tropical
paradise), although Shakespeare speaks of palm trees in other plays.

Clemen, too, seems to want to impose a tropical lushness on the island that the imagery does not completely support. He notes: "We all
of us are aware of the strong earthy atmosphere pervading the play.
Except for *A Midsummer Night's Dream* and *King Lear* there is no
other play of Shakespeare's in which so many plants, fruits and animals appear." Clemen must also note, however, that the plants and animals in *The Tempest* are "mostly brought into relation with physical
pain, threats of punishment, trouble and distress." This problem he
subsumes under the statement, "Compared to the nature-world of *A
Midsummer Night's Dream* . . . the world of flora and fauna in *The Tempest* is less lovely, less 'Elizabethan,' less poetic and aesthetic." This, it
would seem, is putting it mildly. Clemen feels, however, that the impression of "hostile and adverse forces which either oppose man or are
called up against him" is completely superseded "in the fourth act . . .
by the praise of the fruitbearing blessings of nature." In his discussion
of imagery, Clemen makes almost no distinction between the imagery
that refers to the island itself and the imagery that refers to other
places. He praises the "sensuous exuberance and pregnant wealth of
imagery" in Iris' "Ceres, most bounteous lady" speech as if the "rich

leas" of that passage referred to the island. In fact, however, the point of Iris' lengthy message could be paraphrased, "Ceres, Juno bids you leave your fertile and abundant fields to come to this bare island where there is nothing but uncultivated grass." Clemen concludes Iris' message after the beautiful catalogue of images, trailing off with three well-placed dots just before Iris says, "the queen o' th' sky . . . bids thee leave these" (IV.i.70, 72). ⟨ . . . ⟩

In fact, the imagery of the masque seems to constitute a direct contrast to the imagery used in regard to Prospero's island. The following items mentioned in the masque all have to do with *cultivation,* by which I mean Nature organized and controlled by human effort: "wheat," "rye," "barley," "vetches," "oats," "pease," "nibbling sheep," "broom-groves," "poll-clipt vineyard," "barns and garners never empty," "vines with clustring bunches growing," "sunburnt sicklemen," "furrow," and, above all, "harvest." On the other hand, there is no evidence whatsoever to show that there is any kind of cultivation or domestication of animals on the island. Prospero and company seem to have been living on fresh-brook mussels and whatever fish Caliban could trap in his dams. For all that has been said in favor of Prospero's "art" as symbolizing civilization, it seems that in twelve years on the island he has succeeded in establishing no more than what anthropologists would call a "hunting and gathering economy."

There is a purpose to the harvest imagery in the marriage masque. The purpose is to link harvest and marriage, Ceres and Juno, crop fertility and marriage fertility, in proper mythological fashion. It is *not* to contribute to the general "earthy atmosphere" of Prospero's island. The atmosphere of Prospero's island is something quite different, and the language used for the one as opposed to the language used for the other reflects and underlines that difference.

What does Shakespeare actually tell us about the island, and what are the stylistic features of his descriptions? Let us begin by trying to construct a sort of ecological picture of the island as Shakespeare has presented it to us in his play.

The most general descriptions of the island are all quite unflattering: "this most desolate isle" (Ariel, III.iii.80); "this bare island" (Prospero, Epilogue, 8); and "this fearful country" (Gonzalo, V.i.106). One of the earliest general descriptions is ambivalent, showing that one's view of the island really depends on whether one is disposed towards optimism or pessimism, but the description as a whole indicates that at least on this part of the island there is little to provoke comment besides wind and grass:

Adrian.	Though this island seem to be desert,— . . .
	Uninhabitable and almost inaccessible,—
	It must needs be of subtle, tender, and delicate
	temperance . . .
	The air breathes upon us here most sweetly.
Sebast.	As if it had lungs and rotten ones.
Anton.	Or as 'twere perfum'd by a fen.
Gonzalo.	Here is everything advantageous to life.
Anton.	True, save means to live.
Sebast.	Of that there's none, or little.
Gonzalo.	How lush and lusty the grass looks! How green!
Anton.	The ground indeed is tawny.
Sebast.	With an eye of green in't.
Anton.	He misses not much.
Sebast.	No; he doth but mistake the truth totally.

(II.i.35–57)

Indeed, the grassiness and greenness of the island are the only things mentioned by the goddesses in the masque, who refer to the island (or at least the part of the island where the masque takes place) as "this grassplot" (Iris, IV.i.73), "this short-grass'd green" (Ceres, IV.i.83), and "this green land" (Iris, IV.i.130).

The island is fairly large, for it is necessary to have a guide (namely Caliban) to find the fresh springs and fertile places (I.i.338–39; II.ii.164–65; III.ii.73–75). There is some seasonal change, for in his threat to Ariel Prospero measures time in winters (I.ii.296). We know that the coast is cut by coves or nooks, since Ariel feels obliged to explain to Prospero in just which nook he chose to hide the ship (Ariel, I.ii.226–29). We know that there are banks, since Ferdinand sits on one to weep (I.ii.389–90). We know from Ariel that the sands are yellow (I.ii.376). We know that there are large rocks with caves in them, for Caliban lives in one of them (I.ii.342–43) and Stephano hides his stolen liquor in another (II.ii.137–38). There are streams and ponds, some fresh (I.ii.339; II.ii.164; III.ii.75) and some polluted (IV.i.182). Such are the larger ecological features of the island.

—L. T. Fitz, "The Vocabulary of the Environment in *The Tempest*." *Shakespeare Quarterly* 26 (1975): pp. 42–44.

[Don Cameron Allen has written extensively on the Renaissance. Among his numerous books are *Image and Meaning:
Metaphoric Traditions in Renaissance Poetry* (1960) and *The
Star-Crossed Renaissance: The Quarrel About Astrology and Its
Influence in England* (1966). In the excerpt below from his
book, *Image and Meaning, Metaphoric Traditions in Renaissance Poetry,* Allen discusses *The Tempest* as Shakespeare's last
brilliant poem which successfully weds the world of experience with world of dreams and imagination.]

Though *The Tempest* is a play, it is also a complicated masque or a
narrative poem with lyric intervals. It is difficult to compare with
Shakespeare's other plays, for it is briefer, more elaborate in fantasy,
and in some respects more intensely personal than they. During the
last century, it was thought to be confessional and Prospero's final
speeches were associated with Shakespeare's retirement from the theater. The play does not permit this conclusion. Shakespeare is not for-
saking his art. If *The Tempest* is to be read biographically at all, it must
be seen as a poetic summary of the poet's life and its satisfactory
achievements, as the poetic rendering of that bright moment allowed
to men of special favor, a moment that assures them that what they
have loved will endure. *The Tempest,* like *Pericles, Cymbeline,* and *The
Winter's Tale,* is one of a series of warm afternoons in the late autumn
of Shakespeare's life. It is mellow with the ripeness of knowledge, for
its maker has discovered the right ritual for the marriage of the inner
and the outer world, of the real and the ideal, the experienced and the
imagined, the dream and the actuality.

With the writing of *Hamlet* Shakespeare begins to experiment with
darkness, and the sun does not come out again until Pericles, who is
"music's master," hears, like no other character in Shakespeare's plays,
the harmony of the heavenly spheres. This is the same harmonious end
toward which Prospero looks: "When I have required / Some heavenly
music—which even now I do." It is plain from the tragedies that an
awakening from idealism into cold reality is the required preliminary
experience to the search for celestial harmony. The distaste for life expressed by Hamlet, a distaste that helps to shape the succeeding
tragedies, has been associated by biographical critics with the poet's

private experience, with his increasing boredom with life and art, with an obsessing puritanical temper, with a disappointment in love or friendship, and with some sort of neurotic illness. None of this can be proved. All we know is that Shakespeare experimented with tragedy and tragic despair; then, using the same sets of tragic circumstances, he led his creatures out of the world of darkness into eternal day. ⟨ . . . ⟩

The Tempest, like the other last plays, is separated from the world of the Elizabethans by an imaginative reach that is greater than the finite measurements of space and time. It is remote in time and it is out of time. The imaginative distances are enhanced by the mortal chronology of the text: the precise three hours of action and of the twelve-year island sojourn of Prospero and Miranda. Because of these exact statements the interior distance between us and the island is closer than are the external distances of time and space. We can almost find the island in the atlas of literary tradition: it is on or off the direct course to Carthage or Tunis, the capes where Aeneas, swept by storm, came into the realm of "widow Dido." The time may be any time, but it is more truly a constant present. All of these distinctions are made certain by the past, for it is not just that Shakespeare was an Englishman or read the sea adventures of Jourdan that put the island on the chart of his imagination.

We stand, at the play's beginning, watching a storm that we also see through the eyes of Prospero, the stormmaker, and of the admirable Miranda. It is a fairy storm, real only to the men returning from Carthage and to the spellbound girl. It is a storm similar to the one that Prospero may have known inwardly when twelve years before he and his infant daughter crossed the same waters on "a rotten carcass of a butt."

> There they hoist us,
> To cry to the seas, that roared to us; to sigh
> To the winds, whose pity sighing back again
> Did us but loving wrong.

The storm that was then in Prospero's mind was not unlike the one that drove Lear mad, but now, except for occasional ripples of anger or impatience, it has blown itself out. Prospero has been tested and educated in his island; he has learned to control his passions' weather and so he can makes storms in semblance. When Miranda asks how they came ashore, Prospero, grateful for the experience, can give her a serene answer, "By Providence divine." To reach this emotional shelter, one must pass through stormy weather to an island, and it is on the island, outside of known reality, that a symbolic miracle can occur.

To come across broad waters in a helpless boat and to find haven at last in a magic land is a symbolic motif that has found a place in the history of heroes since literature began. The storms that drove the Argonauts are poetically recorded; we know in the same way the wracking tumult in which Ceyx drowned and the monstrous gale that brought Aeneas to Carthage. The accounts of the poets are sustained by the romantic historians, one of whom, Diodorus Siculus, gives us the tale of Iambulus, storm-driven for months in the Erythraean Sea and brought at last to an island where men lived happily in the earliest of Utopias. The same romancer, in his book of islands, sets down a legend congenial with that of *The Tempest*. He writes that sailors from Carthage, exploring the sea beyond the Pillars of Hercules, were carried by strong winds far into the ocean. After many days, they were driven onto an island filled with springs, rivers, and beautiful orchards but unknown to men. Its climate was so felicitous that "it would appear . . . that it was a dwelling-place of gods." But the master of storm, of shipwreck, and of enchanted islands is the wise son of Laertes, Odysseus of many counsels. To understand part of the tradition behind *The Tempest*, we should rehearse his Mediterranean journeys and understand what they mean.

—Don Cameron Allen, *Image and Meaning, Metaphoric Traditions in Renaissance Poetry* (Baltimore: Johns Hopkins Press, 1960): pp. 42–52.

THEODORE SPENCER ON SHAKESPEARE'S VISION OF NATURE

[Theodore Spencer (1902–1949) is the author of *Death and Elizabethan Tragedy* and *Studies in Metaphysical Poetry: Two Essays and a Bibliography.* In the following excerpt, Spencer discusses *The Tempest* in terms of Shakespeare's new imaginative vision of Nature and the individual value of human beings within the context of the time in which he lived.]

The Tempest carries the theme a step further, and it is tempting to see in this last of Shakespeare's complete plays both his final treatment of the difference between appearance and reality and his final presentation, transformed by a new imaginative vision, of the three levels in Nature's hierarchy—the sensible, the rational, and the intellectual—which formed the common psychological assumption of his time. If we succumbed to that temptation, we would claim that the play shows a temporary, apparent, evil dispelled by a lasting, real, good, and that Caliban represents the level of sense, the various noblemen the untrustworthy level of reason, and Prospero with his servant Ariel, the level of uncontaminated intellect. *The Tempest* might thus be made the final piece in an ordered pattern of fully developed insight, a dramatization, based on a new interpretation of Nature's distinctions, of a final vision of redemption and the triumph of goodness.

But the play itself, like all of Shakespeare's work, like human life, defies any scheme so neat and so mechanical. The common assumptions are no doubt present, a part of the texture, but the play is very far from being a mere illustration of them. The characters and the action have a more individual value, hence a more universal significance, than could be given them as mere illustrations of a scheme. Nor can we say, as Prospero returns to his kingdom and Miranda is united to Ferdinand, that there is any universal triumph of goodness. Evil beings incorrigibly still exist, though they are no longer in control nor at the center; the center is edged with darkness, though our eyes may be directed to the central light of transfiguration and restoration. In a world of recreated and newly abandoned relationships there is still a silent Antonio who scowls alone.

Yet, though there is nothing mechanical about their presentation, the familiar levels of value do exist in the play, and to be aware of them may help us to understand it. Caliban, complicated character that he is, does primarily represent the animal level; the "beast Caliban," as Prospero calls him, is a thing "not honor'd with human shape" (I.ii.283); he is set apart—as it were abstracted—from human nature. We are no longer in the climate of tragedy, where human beings themselves are seen as animals, like the Spartan dog Iago or the wolfish daughters of Lear. Though he gives a hint of reformation at the end, Caliban, in Prospero's eyes, is unimprovable; he cannot be tamed by reason; he is

> A devil, a born devil, on whose nature
> Nurture will never stick; on whom my pains
> Humanely taken, are all lost, quite lost.
>   (IV.i.188)

And it is characteristic of him that he should take Stephano, the lowest available specimen of human nature, for a god.

The human beings on Prospero's island are a various crew, perhaps deliberately chosen to present as wide a range as possible. Stephano and Trinculo are Shakespeare's last clowns, representing the laughable, amorally lovable, and quite unchangeable level of human nature; they are appropriately associated with Caliban. Antonio is the rigid, selfish schemer, an egotistic isolationist, cut off from all concerns but his own; Alonzo and Sebastian are also schemers, equally selfish but not as coldly self-centered as Antonio. There is Gonzalo, the testy and amiable official servant of goodness and order, the last of Shakespeare's old men, and there is Ferdinand, the ideal son and prince, the appropriate mate for Miranda, the "wonder" of the island who, like the heroines of the other last plays, is a symbol of unspoilt humanity. Most of these people, with the important and significant exception of the worst and the best, go through some kind of punishment or purgation. The low characters, Stephano and Trinculo, are merely punished, physically: they get befouled and belabored, as is appropriate—the stuff they are made of must be beaten into shape, it lacks the deeper awareness necessary for purgation. But the courtly figures, Alonzo, Antonio, and Sebastian, *are* subjected to purgation. They lose their human faculties for a time, their brains are useless, "boiled" within their skulls; "ignorant fumes . . . mantle their clearer reason," until finally

> their understanding
> Begins to swell, and the approaching tide
> Will shortly fill the reasonable shores
> That now lie foul and muddy.
>   (V.i.79 ff.)

Prospero, until he drowns his book, is clearly on a level above that of ordinary human nature, and though it would be an error to think of him as a representative of purely intellectual capacity, his use of magic is a way of making his superiority dramatically effective; the elves and demi-puppets that have been his agents were considered in certain contemporary circles of thought to be creatures above man in the hierarchy of Nature, between men and angels. Prospero's command of them obviously involves a more than human power. Yet Prospero gives up this power and returns to the human level again. He is purged, but his purgation is exactly opposite to the purgation of Alonzo: Alonzo sinks *below* reason before returning to it; before

Prospero returns to the rational human level he has lived for a time *above* it. The important thing to notice is his return. I cannot agree with those critics who say that Prospero at the end of the play, "finds himself immeasurably nearer than before to the impassivity of the gods," "His theurgical operations," says Mr. Curry, "have accomplished their purpose. He wishes now to take the final step and to consummate the assimilation of his soul to the gods. And this step is to be accomplished through prayer."

But this is clearly a misinterpretation of Shakespeare's meaning. Prospero abjures his magic not to become like the gods, but to return to humanity.

> —Theodore Spencer, *Shakespeare and the Nature of Man* (New York: Macmillan Co., 1969): pp. 195–198.

JONATHAN BATE ON CALABAN AND COLONIAL OPPRESSION

[Jonathan Bate is the author of *Shakespeare and the English Romantic Imagination* and *The Genius of Shakespeare* (1998). In the excerpt below, Bate discusses how the play should be classified and provides some historical background on colonial America and Caliban's representation as an enslaved victim of colonial oppression.]

To describe *The Tempest* as a metaphoric romance is to beg the question of its generic classification. The compilers of the first folio placed it first among Shakespeare's comedies, while twentieth-century criticism has grouped it among the so-called late romances. Both generic terms would have been recognizable to a Jacobean audience, although the latter one was not usually applied to the drama. *The Tempest* shares with Shakespeare's earlier comedies a movement towards reconciliation and marriage, together with a sense of disaster averted. As Don John's conspiracy fails in *Much Ado About Nothing,* so the various conspiracies against Prospero fail in *The Tempest;* the play ends, in the traditional fashion of comedy, with the young lovers united, but also, like all Shakespearian comedies, with certain ends left untied—Antonio does not speak to Prospero when the elder brother offers him grudging forgiveness; the sense of exclusion recapitulates the way in which Shakespeare's earlier Antonios stand apart from the resolutions in marriage at the end of *The Merchant of Venice* and *Twelfth Night*. As for romance, *The Tempest* shares with *Pericles* sea-voyages and storm, lost children, magical transformations and revivals—all features of the romance form which may be traced back through medieval figures like Gower, the narrator of *Pericles,* to Hellenistic sources such as the tale of Apollonius of Tyre, which lies distantly behind not only *Pericles* but also the romance element of *The Comedy of Errors.* ⟨ . . . ⟩

The Virginia Company was established by royal charter in 1606, the Jamestown Colony set up in 1607. In 1609 several hundred potential new colonists ran into a storm near the Virginia coast; the ship of Sir Thomas Gates, the governor, was driven to Bermuda, where it landed safely and the voyagers were able to winter. It has long been recognized that William Strachey's eyewitness account of these events is the likely source for various details in the play, though Shakespeare would have had to see the 'Strachey letter' in manuscript, since it was not published until 1625. Several allusions give the play a New World aura. Few audience members could have missed the resonance of Miranda's "O brave new world," ironic as her wonder is in context. Ariel links the tempest to the New World with his reference to the "still-vexed Bermudas." Caliban's god Setebos is a Patagonian deity, mentioned in Magellan's voyages; the name Caliban itself inevitably suggests "cannibal" and thus a certain image of New World savages. Prospero's enslavement of Caliban seems to be a stage-image of colonial oppression—in particular, his use of language as a method of control is, according to Stephen Greenblatt in his influential essay "Learning to Curse," a classic strategy of colonialism. Trinculo apprehends Caliban as a bizarre creature who may be exploited for financial gain: "Were I in England now, as once I was, and had but this fish painted, not a holiday-fool there but would give a piece of silver. There would this monster make a man—any strange beast there makes a man. When they will not give a doit to relieve a lame beggar, they will lay out ten to see a dead Indian." The idea is explained by Frank Kermode in a laconic footnote: "Such exhibitions were a regular feature of colonial policy under James I. The exhibits rarely survived the experience."

The text also draws on more positive images of the New World: the island is rich in natural produce and may thus be read as a virgin land—a Virginia—ripe with Utopian possibilities. So it is that Gonzalo lifts from Montaigne's essay "Of the Caniballes" a Utopian vision of what he would do if he had the "plantation" (the word denotes the right to colonize) of the isle. Montaigne inverted the normative view of the relationship between "civilized" and "savage," arguing that the inhabitants of the "new world" of the Americas were the truly civilized ones since they were closer to "their originall naturalitie" and "the lawes of nature" than are the Europeans. "It is a nation," he wrote in a sentence closely imitated by Shakespeare,

> that hath no kind of trafficke, no knowledge of Letters, no intelligence of numbers, no name of magistrate, nor of politike superioritie; no use of service, of riches or of povertie; no contracts, no successions, no partitions, no occupation but idle; no respect of kinred, but common, no apparrell but naturall, no manuring of lands, no use of wine, corne, or mettle.

That Shakespeare read Montaigne's wide-ranging critique of European assumptions about the inferiority of "barbarians" prior to writing *The Tempest* is the most compelling piece of evidence in support of the view that the play is a troubled exploration of imperial and colonial strategies. Montaigne and Shakespeare have thus come to the assistance of post-colonial critics who for good reasons need to work through their own guilt about these matters.

But there are problems with a New World reading. Caliban's god may be of the New World, but his mother, a much more important figure, is from the old world: apparently Prospero considers it necessary to remind Ariel once a month that she was born in Algiers. Caliban himself is not a native inhabitant of the island: he is the child of the Algerian Sycorax who was herself an earlier exile to the island. Prospero is not establishing an empire, he is exiled to a place that is thought to be barren. The play is not at all interested in the things that colonization is primarily interested in: gold, spices, tobacco. And the location of the island is not the New World, but what was for the Elizabethans the centre of the old world, the Mediterranean; Shakespeare is careful to inform his audience that the shipwreck occurs *en route* from Tunis to Naples.

—Jonathan Bate, *Critical Essays on Shakespeare's The Tempest* (New York: G.K. Hall & Co., 1998): pp. 39–42.

[Stephen Jay Greenblatt is the author of *Representing the English Renaissance* and *Marvelous Possessions: The Wonder of the New World*. In the excerpt below, Greenblatt discusses Prospero's role as the creator and manager of anxiety in *The Tempest* by focusing on the ways in which he manipulates and "refashions" the identity of the other characters.]

When near the close of his career Shakespeare reflected upon his own art with still greater intensity and self-consciousness than in *Measure for Measure*, he once again conceived of the playwright as a princely creator of anxiety. But where in *Measure for Measure* disguise is the principle emblem of this art, in *The Tempest* the emblem is the far more potent and disturbing power of magic. Prospero's chief magical activity throughout *The Tempest* is to harrow the other characters with fear and wonder and then to reveal that their anxiety is his to create and allay. The spectacular storm in the play's first scene gives way to Miranda's empathic agitation: "O! I have suffered / With those that I saw suffer. . . . O, the cry did knock / Against my very heart." "The direful spectacle of the wrack," replies Prospero,

> which touch'd
> The very virtue of compassion in thee,
> I have with such provision in mine art
> So safely ordered that there is no soul—
> No, not so much perdition as an hair
> Betid to any creature in the vessel
> Which thou heardst cry, which thou saw'st sink.
> (1.2.26–32)

Miranda has been treated to an intense experience of suffering and to a still more intense demonstration of her father's power, the power at once to cause such suffering and to cancel it. Later in the play the threat of "perdition"—both loss and damnation—will be concentrated against Prospero's enemies, but it is important to recall that at the start the management of anxiety through the "provision" of art is practiced upon Prospero's beloved daughter. Her suffering is the prelude to the revelation of her identity, as if Prospero believes that this revelation can be meaningful only in the wake of the amazement and pity he artfully arouses. He is setting out to fashion her identity, just as he is setting out to refashion the inner lives of his enemies, and he employs comparable disciplinary techniques.

With his daughter, Prospero's techniques are mediated and softened: she suffers at the sight of the sufferings of unknown wretches. With his enemies the techniques are harsher and more direct—the spectacle they are compelled to watch is not the wreck of others but of their own lives. In one of the play's most elaborate scenes, Prospero stands above the stage, invisible to those below him, and conjures up a banquet for Alonso, Antonio, Sebastian, and their party; when they move toward the table, Ariel appears like a Harpy and, with a clap of his wings and a burst of thunder and lightning, makes the table disappear. Ariel then solemnly recalls their crimes against Prospero and sentences the guilty in the name of the powers of Destiny and Fate:

> Thee of thy son, Alonso,
> They have bereft; and do pronounce by me
> Ling'ring perdition (worse than any death
> Can be at once).
>
> (3.3.75–78)

Prospero is delighted at Ariel's performance:

> My high charms work,
> And these, mine enemies, are all knit up
> In their distractions. They now are in my pow'r.
>
> (3.3.88–90)

To compel others to be "all knit up / In their distractions," to cause a paralyzing anxiety, is the dream of power, a dream perfected over bitter years of exile. But as we have already seen, the artful manipulation of anxiety is not only the manifestation of aggression; it is also a strategy for shaping the inner lives of others and for fashioning their behavior. Hence we find Prospero employing the strategy not only upon those he hates but upon his daughter and upon the man whom he has chosen to be his daughter's husband. Ferdinand and Miranda fall in love instantly—"It goes on, I see, / As my soul prompts it" (1.2.420–21), remarks Prospero—but what is missing from their love is precisely the salutary anxiety that Prospero undertakes to impose: "this swift business / I must uneasy make, lest too light winning / Make the prize light" (1.2.451–53). To Miranda's horror, he accuses Ferdinand of treason and employs his magic charms once again to cause a kind of paralysis: "My spirits," exclaims Ferdinand, "as in a dream, are all bound up" (1.2.487). The rituals of humiliation and suffering through which Prospero makes Ferdinand and Miranda pass evidently have their desired effect: at the end of the play the couple displayed to the amazed bystanders are revealed to be not only in a state of love but in a state of symbolic war. The lovers, you will recall, are discovered playing chess, and Miranda accuses Ferdinand of cheating. The deepest happiness is represented in this play as a state of playful tension.

Perhaps the supreme representation of this tension in *The Tempest* is to be found not in Prospero's enemies or in his daughter and son-in-law but in himself. The entire action of the play rests on the premise that value lies in controlled uneasiness, and hence that a direct reappropriation of the usurped dukedom and a direct punishment of the usurpers has less moral and political value than an elaborate inward restaging of loss, misery, and anxiety. Prospero directs this restaging not only against the others but also—even principally—against himself. That is, he arranges for the reenactment in a variety of registers and through different symbolic agents of the originary usurpation, and in the play's most memorable yet perplexing moment, the princely artist puts himself through the paralyzing uneasiness with which he has afflicted others.

—Stephen Jay Greenblatt, *Shakespearean Negotiations: The Circulation of Social Energy in Renaissance England* (Berkeley: University of California Press, 1988): pp. 142–144.

John Dover Wilson on Shakespeare's Retirement

[John Dover Wilson (1881–1969) was a very well known scholar who wrote extensively on Shakespeare. Among his books are *The Elizabethan Shakespeare* (1970) and *An Introduction to the Sonnets of Shakespeare for the Use of Historians and Others* (1964). In the following excerpt, Wilson applies biographical background on the circumstances of Shakespeare's retirement from London in 1612 to his discussion of *The Tempest* as the imaginative triumph of the playwright's farewell to theatre.]

Many writers assume that Shakespeare was more or less of a convalescent in his last years, that his grip was loosening and his brain softening. I can see no evidence whatever for this in the plays themselves. Turning to invent a new form of drama to match a new mood, Shakespeare as usual experiments before he achieves exactly what he aims at, and by the side of *The Tempest* its immediate predecessors, it is true, seem loose-knit. Yet they are lovely things in themselves—*Cymbeline*, it must be remembered, was Tennyson's favourite play, and his precious copy was buried with him; while *The Tempest*, as a piece of sheer artistry, is surely the most consummate of all Shakespeare's masterpieces. But why did not Shakespeare write anything after *The Tempest*? Is there not something odd, enquires the Shylock school of criticism, in a man giving up a lucrative profession at the age of forty-eight, leaving London at the height of his fame, and retiring to an obscure provincial town like Stratford? And there follows talk of Bright's disease, or even worse things are whispered.

The problem of the retirement is, as I shall later show, closely related to that of the "conversion." But two things may be said at once about it. In the first place, the break with London in 1612 was clearly deliberate, and a decision taken when Shakespeare was apparently in perfect health. *The Tempest* proves this; for *The Tempest*, as most readers have agreed, is on the face of it Shakespeare's farewell to the theatre, and *The Tempest* was not written by a sick man. And in the second place, there is not a hint either in contemporary record or local tradition that Shakespeare suffered disability or disease of any sort during his later years. On the contrary, all we can glean points to cheerfulness and happiness. His biographer Rowe, writing in 1709, declares that "the latter part of his life was spent, as all men of good sense will wish theirs may be, in ease, retirement, and the conversation of friends," while he also asserts that Shakespeare was well acquainted with many gentlemen of the neighbourhood. There were visitors too from London. We are told of a convivial meeting with Drayton and Ben Jonson shortly before the end, which does not suggest failing health and certainly suggests high spirits. The information comes from John Ward, vicar of Stratford from 1662 to 1681, who adds "it seems" that they "drank too hard, for Shakespeare died of a fever there contracted." The supposition of the parson we may discount, like the tale of dying a papist. But we have no reason to disbelieve his statement about the "fever"; many in Stratford as early as 1662 would remember what the great man died of, and Ward who was interested in medicine would take careful note of such a fact. Shakespeare, we may therefore assume, was carried off by some epidemic four years after he had turned his back upon London.

To understand Shakespeare's retirement, we must return to 1608, try and fathom his "conversion," and study his last plays. For here as in everything else about him the poet was father to the man, and Keats is the truest guide when he tells us that "Shakespeare led a life of allegory; his works are the comments upon it."

As I have said, sickness of the body as well as sickness of spirit there may well have been after the completion of *Lear,* but illness is not necessary to explain the lifting of the clouds in *Antony and Cleopatra,* the ebb of the tragic tide visible in *Coriolanus,* the dawn of a new mood in *Pericles* and *Cymbeline.* And the "conversion" itself is of course a poetic one—none the less real or profound for that! Accordingly we must go for helpful analogies, not to the theological or moral sphere, but to the realm of art. ⟨ . . . ⟩

I use words I wrote about Wordsworth five years ago, without a thought of Shakespeare in my mind. The parallel is not exact, of course; history does not repeat herself. But the crisis and its occasion, the conversion and its cause, are extraordinarily similar. Wordsworth recovered by falling in love a second time with the Lake country; Shakespeare by falling in love a second time with Stratford. But let Wordsworth himself speak for the creator of *Lear.*

> These beauteous forms,
> Through a long absence, have not been to me
> As is a landscape to a blind man's eye:
> But oft, in lonely rooms, and 'mid the din
> Of towns and cities, I have owed to them,
> In hours of weariness, sensations sweet,
> Felt in the blood, and felt along the heart;
> And passing even into my purer mind,
> With tranquil restoration. . . . Nor less, I trust,
> To them I may have owed another gift,
> Of aspect more sublime; that blessed mood,
> In which the burthen of the mystery,
> In which the heavy and the weary weight
> Of all this unintelligible world,
> Is lightened:—that serene and blessed mood
> In which the affections gently lead us on,—
> Until, the breath of this corporeal frame
> And even the motion of our human blood

Almost suspended, we are laid asleep
In body, and become a living soul:
While with an eye made quiet by the power
Of harmony, and the deep power of joy,
We see into the life of things.

There is no more wonderful description of poetic ecstasy in all poetry than this, and there is no better illustration of its truth than *The Tempest.* Wordsworth explains the last plays of Shakespeare, and the last plays lend to Wordsworth's lines the force of a new revelation.

Shakespeare fell in love with Stratford, with its memories, its quiet pastures and wide skies, with all the wild life of bird and beast and flower, with his pleasant friendships and domesticities of the little town, with his house and garden, with his own family, and especially perhaps with his younger daughter.

—John Dover Wilson, *The Essential Shakespeare* (Cambridge: Cambridge University Press, 1932): pp. 131–133, 135–137.

Works by William Shakespeare

Venus and Adonis. 1593.

The Rape of Lucrece. 1594.

Henry VI. 1594.

Titus Andronicus. 1594.

The Taming of the Shrew. 1594.

Romeo and Juliet. 1597.

Richard III. 1597.

Richard II. 1597.

Love's Labour's Lost. 1598.

Henry IV. 1598.

The Passionate Pilgrim. 1599.

A Midsummer Night's Dream. 1600.

The Merchant of Venice. 1600.

Much Ado About Nothing. 1600.

Henry V. 1600.

The Phoenix and the Turtle. 1601.

The Merry Wives of Winsor. 1602.

Hamlet. 1603.

King Lear. 1608.

Troilus and Cressida. 1609.

Sonnets. 1609.

Pericles. 1609.

Othello. 1622.

Mr. William Shakespeares Comedies, Histories & Tragedies. Ed. John Heminge and Henry Condell. 1623 (First Folio), 1632 (Second Folio), 1663 (Third Folio), 1685 (Fourth Folio).

Poems. 1640.

Works. Ed. Nicholas Rowe. 1709. 6 vols.

Works. Ed. Alexander Pope. 1723–25, 6 vols.

Works. Ed. Lewis Theobald. 1733. 7 vols.

Works. Ed. Thomas Hanmer. 1743–44. 6 vols.

Works. Ed. William Warburton. 1747. 8 vols.

Plays. Ed. Samuel Johnson. 1765. 8 vols.

Plays and Poems. Ed. Edmond Malone. 1790. 10 vols.

The Family Shakespeare. Ed. Thomas Bowdler. 1807. 4 vols.

Works. Ed. J. Payne Collier. 1842–44. 8 vols.

Works. Ed. H. N. Hudson. 1851–56. 11 vols.

Works. Ed. Alexander Dyce. 1857. 6 vols.

Works. Ed. Richard Grant White. 1857–66. 12 vols.

Works (Cambridge Edition). Ed. William George Clark, John Glover, and William Aldis Wright. 1863–66. 9 vols.

A New Variorum Edition of the Works of Shakespeare. Ed. H. H. Furness et al. 1871–.

Works. Ed. W. J. Rolfe. 1871–96. 40 vols.

The Pitt Press Shakespeare. Ed. A. W. Verity. 1890–1905. 13 vols.

The Warwick Shakespeare. 1893–1938. 13 vols.

The Temple Shakespeare. Ed. Israel Gollancz. 1894–97. 40 vols.

The Arden Shakespeare. Ed W. J. Craig, R. H. Case et al. 1899–1924. 37 vols.

The Shakespeare Apocrypha. Ed. C. F. Tucker Brooke. 1908.

The Yale Shakespeare. Ed. Wilbur L. Cross, Tucker Brooke, and Willard Highley Durham. 1912–27. 40 vols.

The New Shakespeare (Cambridge Edition). Ed. Arthur Quiller-Couch and John Dover Wilson. 1921–62. 38 vols.

The New Temple Shakespeare. Ed. M. R. Ridley. 1934–36. 39 vols.

Works. Ed. George Lyman Kittredge. 1936.

The Penguin Shakespeare. Ed. G. B. Harrison. 1937–59. 36 vols.

The New Clarendon Shakespeare. Ed. R. E. C. Houghton. 1938–.

The Arden Shakespeare. Ed. Una Ellis-Fermor et al. 1951–.

The Complete Pelican Shakespeare. Ed. Alfred Harbage. 1969.

The Complete Signet Classic Shakespeare. Ed. Sylvan Barnet. 1972.

The Oxford Shakespeare. Ed. Stanley Wells. 1982–.

The New Cambridge Shakespeare. Ed. Philip Brockbank. 1984–.

Works about
Shakespeare's Romances

Adams, Robert. *Shakespeare: The Four Romances.* New York: Hill, 1973.

Nicoll, Allardyce. *Shakespeare.* London: Methuen, 1952.

Beresford-Howe, Constance. *Prospero's Daughter.* Toronto: Macmillan, 1987.

Bergeron, David M. *Shakespeare's Romances and the Royal Family.* Lawrence: University Press of Kansas, 1985.

Brockbank, Philip, editor. *Players of Shakespeare: Essays in Shakespearean Performance by Twelve Players with the Royal Shakespeare Company.* Cambridge; New York: Cambridge University Press, 1985.

Bush, Geoffrey. *Shakespeare and the Natural Condition.* Cambridge: Harvard University Press, 1956.

Cawley, R.R. *Voyagers and Elizabethan Drama.* Boston: D.C. Heath, 1938.

————. *Unpathed Waters: Studies in the Influence of Voyagers on Elizabethan Literature.* Princeton, N.J., 1940.

Chambers, E.K. *Shakespeare: A Survey.* New York: Hill and Wang, 1958.

Craig, Hardin. *An Interpretation of Shakespeare.* New York: Citadel, 1948.

Curry, W.C. *Shakespeare's Philosophical Patterns.* Baton Rouge: Louisiana State University Press, 1959.

Cutts, John P. *Rich and Strange: A Study of Shakespeare's Last Plays.* Pullman: Washington State University Press, 1968.

Danby, John F. *Poets on Fortune's Hill: Studies in Sidney, Shakespeare, Beaumont and Fletcher.* London: Faber and Faber, 1952.

Driver, Tom. *The Sense of History in Greek and Shakespearean Drama.* New York: Columbia University Press, 1960.

Faber, M.D., comp. *The Design Within: Psychoanalytic Approaches to Shakespeare.* New York: Science House, 1970.

Farnham, Willard. *The Shakespearean Grotesque: Its Genesis and Transformations.* Oxford: Clarendon Press, 1971.

Felperin, Howard. *Shakespearean Romance.* Princeton: Princeton University Press, 1972.

Fergusson, Francis. *Shakespeare: The Pattern in His Carpet.* New York: Delacorte, 1958.

Forker, Charles R. *Fancy's Images: Contexts, Settings, and Perspectives in Shakespeare and His Contemporaries.* Carbondale: Southern Illinois University Press, 1990.

Foakes, F.A. *Shakespeare: The Dark Comedies to the Last Plays – From Satire to Celebration.* Charlottesville: University Press of Virginia, 1971.

Frey, Charles. *Shakespeare's Vast Romance: A Study of* The Winter's Tale. Columbia: University of Missouri Press, 1980.

Frye, Northrop. *A Natural Perspective: The Development of Shakespearean Comedy and Romance.* New York: Columbia University Press, 1955. (Reprint) New York: Harcourt, Brace and World, 1965.

Gesner, Carol. *Shakespeare and the Greek Romance.* Lexington: University Press of Kentucky, 1970.

Gittings, Robert, ed. *The Living Shakespeare.* London: Heinemann, 1960.

Hartwig, Joan. *Shakespeare's Tragicomic Vision.* Baton Rouge: Louisiana State University Press, 1972.

Holland, Norman. *Psychoanalysis and Shakespeare.* New York: McGraw Hill, 1966.

———. *The Shakespearean Imagination.* Bloomington and London: Indiana University Press, and New York: MacMillan, 1964.

Hunter, Robert G. *Shakespeare and the Comedy of Forgiveness.* New York: Columbia University Press, 1965.

Kermode, Frank. *Shakespeare, Spenser, Donne: Renaissance Essays.* New York: Viking Press, 1971.

Knight, G. Wilson. *The Crown of Life: Essays in Interpretation of Shakespeare's Final Plays.* London: Oxford University Press, 1947. (Reprint) New York: Barnes And Noble, 1966.

———. *The Shakespearian Tempest.* London: Oxford University Press, 1932. (Reprint) London: Methuen, 1971.

Levin, Harry. *The Myth of the Golden Age in the Renaissance.* Bloomington: Indiana University Press, 1969.

Meader, William Granville. *Courtship in Shakespeare: Its Relation to the Tradition of Courtly Love.* New York: King's Crown Press, Columbia University, 1954.

Mowat, Barbara. *The Dramaturgy of Shakespeare's Romances.* Athens: University of Georgia Press, 1977.

Murphy, Miranda. *The Measure of Miranda.* Edmonton: Newest, 1987.

Nelson, Thomas Allen. *Shakespeare's Comic Theory: A Study of Art and Artifice in the Last Plays.* The Hague and Paris: Mouton, 1972.

Nuttall, Anthony David. *A New Mimesis: Shakespeare and the Representation of Reality.* London; New York: Methuen, 1989.

Peterson, Douglas L. *Time, Tide and Tempest: A Study of Shakespeare's Romances.* San Marino, California: Huntington Library, 1973.

Pettet, E.C. *Shakespeare and the Romance Tradition.* London: Staples Press, 1949.

Phialas, Peter. *Shakespeare's Romantic Comedies: The Development of Their Form and Meaning.* Chapel Hill: University of North Carolina Press, 1966.

Pyle, Fitzroy. *"The Winter's Tale": A Commentary on the Structure.* London: Routledge and Kegan Paul, and New York: Barnes and Noble, 1968.

Simonds, Peggy Muñoz. *Myth, Emblem, and Music in Shakespeare's* Cymbeline: *An Iconographic Reconstruction.* Newark: University of Delaware Press, 1992.

Smith, Hallett. *Shakespeare's Romances: A Study of Some Ways of the Imagination.* San Marino, California: Huntington Library, 1972.

Spencer, Theodore. *Shakespeare and the Nature of Man.* New York: MacMillan Company, 1949.

Summers, Joseph Holmes. *Dreams of Love and Power.* Oxford: Clarendon Press, 1984.

Sundelson, David. *Shakespeare's Restorations of the Father.* New Brunswick: Rutgers University Press, 1983.

Tillyard, E.M.W. *Shakespeare's Last Plays.* London: Chatto and Windus, 1938. (Reprint) 1964.

Tobias, Richard C., and Paul G. Zolbrod, eds. *Shakespeare's Late Plays: Essays in Honor of Charles Crow.* Athens: Ohio University Press, 1974.

Traversi, Derek. *Shakespeare: The Last Phase.* New York: Harcourt, 1955.

Uphaus, Robert W. *Beyond Tragedy: Structure and Experience in Shakespeare's Romances.* Lexington: University of Kentucky, 1981.

Wain, John. *The Living World of Shakespeare: A Playgoer's Guide.* New York: St. Martin's Press, 1964.

Wheeler, Richard P. *Shakespeare's Development and the Problem Comedies: Turn and Counter-turn.* Berkeley and Los Angeles: University of California Press, 1981.

Wilson, John Dover. *The Elizabethan Shakespeare.* London: Folcroft Press, 1970.

Yates, Francis A. *Shakespeare's Last Plays: A New Approach.* London: Routledge and Kegan Paul, 1975.

Young, David P. *The Heart's Forest: A Study of Shakespeare's Pastoral Plays.* New Haven: Yale University Press, 1972.

Index of
Themes and Ideas